I Shall Not Want

A Owen J Howell Jones.

Baptised by Fire 4

I Shall Not Want.

I Shall Not Want

*Living in the Blessings
of Psalm 23*

Andrew Owen

New Wine Press

New Wine Ministries
PO Box 17
Chichester
West Sussex
United Kingdom
PO19 2AW

ISBN 978-1-905991-55-6

Typeset by **documen**, www.documen.co.uk
Cover design by CCD, www.ccdgroup.co.uk
Printed in the United Kingdom

CONTENTS

Introduction

"Take me to your leader" was a comical quip used frequently in old cartoon strips about extra-terrestrials. Should aliens have ever visited planet Earth, it was what we imagined they'd say. Why? Because if we know one thing, it's that everyone has a leader even if we don't realise it. We should then ask – but who is leading you? If someone said to you, "Take me to your leader," who would you point to? When you think about the people you admire and aspire to be like the most, who comes into your mind?

Everyone looks to someone for leadership at some level in their life, so let's ask another question: if you are following someone, do they know about it? And if so, do they care? Are they even interested in you? To them you may just be a client, a fan, a student, an employee or something else. But as important as these relationships are, they don't even come close to the highest form of leadership known to man: *shepherding*. This is what we will be exploring throughout this book.

Psalm 23

Psalm 23 is probably the best known and most frequently quoted psalm in the Bible. It is often read at funerals, but if that is its only purpose then its potential and truth has been missed, because it's all about LIFE. Psalm 23 describes a life that is intended to go places, a life that should and could navigate the upsides and downsides successfully. It is all about making a success of one's life, not just being successful in life.

Throughout the psalm the writer, David, refers to God as his shepherd. In ancient times it was common to refer to the king of a nation as its "shepherd", not merely its leader. In Scripture, David himself is referred to as the "great shepherd of Israel". He rose from humble beginnings and, as he penned this psalm, David was older, maybe much older. He had been there, done it all and got the T-shirt. He was a mighty, seasoned warrior and a king – hugely successful. But he used this psalm to inform his followers, "You may see me as a legendary general and leader, but there is a *great* power behind this throne. I too am a sheep, being led by a greater Shepherd." He goes on to express the enormous comfort, faith, sense of reassurance and hope he possesses because of this truth.

So come with me now on a journey through this psalm, and see what it *could* mean to us personally, as we learn about real leadership, the highest ever known to man, the kind that you will really, truly want to tell others about.

"The Lord is my shepherd;
I shall not want.
He makes me to lie down in green pastures;
He leads me beside the still waters.
He restores my soul;
He leads me in the paths of righteousness
For His name's sake.
Yea, though I walk through the valley of the shadow
of death,

I will fear no evil;
For You are with me;
Your rod and Your staff, they comfort me.
You prepare a table before me in the presence of
my enemies;
You anoint my head with oil;
My cup runs over.
Surely goodness and mercy shall follow me
All the days of my life;
And I will dwell in the house of the LORD
Forever."

(Psalm 23 NKJV)

Andrew Owen
Glasgow, 2010

1 Shepherding – No Higher Form of Leadership Opportunity

David begins this psalm with the words, *"The Lord is my shepherd ..."* He could have equally written, "The Lord is my *leader"*, or how about "The Lord is my *mentor"*, or maybe, "The Lord is my *teacher ... guru ... coach."* In today's world, any one of those could have been acceptable, but that is not what he wrote. He said, "The Lord is my *Shepherd"* and that is exactly what he meant to say.

People assume that David simply wrote from an analogy familiar to him, since he himself had been a shepherd. True, he had, but he had also been a captain, a general, a king, a businessman, an architect, a giant-killer, a poet and a hugely successful singer/songwriter – more people sang his songs than any one else in his day! He could have chosen any one of these analogies then, but instead he chose that of a shepherd.

Shepherding is an entirely different ball game to any kind of leadership you have come across before. Most of us are very familiar with other kinds of leadership. A bank manager told me that her bosses at the bank made a budget available to help her find a mentor. Life-coaching is a growth industry.

Well-heeled kids have coaches for everything from maths to tennis. Business guru books fly off the shelves. But no university has as yet written a curriculum on *"shepherding – the best leadership model"*. Shepherding belongs' to an altogether higher form of life.

In recent years, many Christian leaders have focused on *servant leadership* following, they say, the example of Jesus of Nazareth, who didn't see Himself as a diva, but a friend of the helpless and a hope to the downtrodden. Jesus didn't walk around telling people what to do, but got down and into the proverbial "stuff off the fan" with people and lifted them out of it. Even hugely successful leadership books like Jim Collins' *From Good to Great* demonstrate the power of humility in Fortune 500 captains. But as good and honourable as this is, we are going further. We are going into another orbit when we talk about *shepherding,* because a shepherd will assume a level of responsibility that no leader, mentor, guru or teacher ever will.

Psalm 23 is unique amongst the other psalms because it is so personal. Seventeen times in six short verses we read the words "me", "my" or "I". It begins, "The Lord is *my* shepherd" when it could just have easily been written more objectively: "The Lord is *a* shepherd..." How much more powerful is it to be able to say, *"The Lord is my shepherd"*, denoting a deep and ongoing relationship? It expresses a contract one has entered into. The Lord may be a shepherd, but is he *your* shepherd? If this is true, at what point did this shepherding relationship start and is the contract still running? Since the shepherd assumes responsibilities that no other leader will, He needs to know who's in and who's out. If there is an opportunity to get in on a relationship like this, how do you get in? Are there terms and conditions?

We need to look at all of these things.

According to Jesus, this is also a defining characteristic of all of His followers and His relationship with them. Christ's sheep know His voice. It's personal, it is intimate and it's current.

In this psalm David reveals to us several characteristics of shepherd-type leadership and in so doing makes the potential and possibility of a relationship with God hugely attractive.

A shepherd provides

A shepherd assumes a responsibility to provide for those under his care. Just think about that! Business mentors make no promise of *provision*. If things go wrong, as far as the mentor is concerned they may feel sorry for the person, but it is ultimately *their* business and *their* problem. Coaches will train, push, motivate and encourage you to win, but there are others where you came from! Teachers teach and pass on their knowledge, but hey, it's up to you to pass the exam!

David, on the other hand, was able to say, *"The Lord is my shepherd"* and in the next breath inform us that, *"I shall not want."* His shepherd was far more than a regular leader, teacher or mentor – He had assumed full responsibility for providing for David and David knew it. He not only knew it in his head, but in his everyday life. He could point to days when he was tired, wiped out, undeserving, below par on his performance, even sinful. He could take you to days where he was mad, sad and glad, and he could tell you clearly of days when he least deserved anything – but he still had a shepherd who provided for his needs. When writing this psalm he was not theorising, he was reporting. He is the king in Israel, he's already made it, and he's telling us how! His shepherd-follower relationship was not built on getting what he deserved or what he had worked hard for. It was built on the massive, generous heart of a merciful benefactor, known as The Shepherd. Sheep don't usually shop for shepherds, it starts the other way around. Intriguing? We are so used to living in a meritocracy, getting what we earn or work hard for. The twin towers of our world are hard work and effort. After all, doesn't God help those who help themselves?

In this psalm David does not tell us how to be a good sheep. It's not "5 steps to successful sheep living". It's not about how "to rise above the flock" or "how to increase the grass under your feet". Neither is it written with a "grow greener grass" mindset. In fact, it's hardly about him at all – it's about this Shepherd and the life-changing benefits his followers as sheep get because of the relationship.

A Middle Eastern shepherd would often have a vast flock, maybe thousands of sheep, under his care. Such a large number of animals would not take long to munch their way through all the grass in a field, so it was the shepherd's responsibility to find fresh grazing pasture for them. He had to make sure his sheep were well provided for.

As David had "munched" his way through life and walked through its many traumatic fields, he both reports and predicts, "I shall not want."

A shepherd protects

Listen to this: a shepherd also take responsibility to *protect* those in his care. David rose to prominence in the eyes of the people because, as a young shepherd boy, he killed the mighty warrior Goliath. How did he have the courage to do such a thing? The Bible tells us he *ran* to meet Goliath on that day. He did this while 40,000 other trained troops stood back, afraid to make a move.

The Bible also tells us his confidence came from his experience – the experience of his shepherding work. While needing to defend the sheep in his care he had already killed both lions and bears. While in that potentially life-threatening situation he came through. He did not attribute this success to his prowess in the field, or to the martial arts academy of "lion slaying", but claimed the Lord helped him.

Since David knew the Lord was his Shepherd, he knew that protection would carry over into Goliath territory.

We learn that this Shepherd watches out for us every second of every day, guiding us through moments where we just think we might die in the infamous *valley of the shadow of death* experience. But this is not a reference to death, as there is a lot more life spoken about after it. Shouldn't that give us great reassurance? When you know that God is in control of your life, it takes away all the anxiety and pressure.

> *"It is better to trust in the LORD than to put your confidence in man."*
>
> (Psalm 118:8)

A shepherd assumes responsibility to lead

Is your life going places? Is it even going anywhere? Leaders lead – that is what they do! As Shepherding is the best form of leadership, it's only natural to expect it to give us the best form of direction! He leads and we follow. We are talking about BIG issues like vision, purpose and meaning. We are talking about the very reason we get up in the morning.

God doesn't want us to stumble through life, muddling through and trying to make the best of it – He wants to lead us forward on a path of purpose and significance. This shepherd has an opinion on our choices because He wants to take us places.

I love Jeremiah's prophecy that says,

" 'For I know the plans I have for you,' declares the
LORD, 'plans to prosper you and not to harm you, plans
to give you hope and a future'"
(Jeremiah 29:11 NIV).

Jesus of Nazareth also referred to himself as a *shepherd leader*. He said, *"I am the good Shepherd."*

The statement "Follow me" was the beginning of the "shepherding contract" between Jesus and His followers. Once they had said "yes" to His invitation then He assumed responsibility for them and they were under His care.

Remember the occasion when the disciples thought their boat was going to sink in a storm? They cried out, "Jesus, don't you care?!" His answer was, "Where is your faith?" Then He spoke out and stilled the wind and the waves. The point that Jesus was making by questioning their faith was simply this: "You have said you will follow Me. So why have you stopped trusting that I will take care of you?"

I find it quite amazing that God Almighty wants to lead me. Does He really have time for that? Is He even aware of me? Consider the enormity and awesomeness of His character and nature. This is God eternal, who existed before time, who has watched kingdoms come and go, who has seen millions of people live and die – and He cares enough about you and me to take a personal interest in our lives! He wants to shepherd us and get intimately involved with us. How often do we look out for His leading and agree it's a great idea to follow Him? How do you even pick up the trail?

A shepherd assumes responsibility to intervene

People sometimes say to us, "Call me if you need me" – a great invitation you might think. But often times we don't feel like calling, so we don't. Or we might doubt the sincerity of the invitation: "They mean well, but they tell everybody that." Or maybe we don't want to call someone just in case we get the third degree because we know we've messed up?

But the Shepherd will turn up, step in and intervene – not as some unannounced inspector of lives, but armed with a "rod and staff", which according to David are designed to comforted us. Once, while travelling through a war zone in central Africa, our party was constantly accompanied by an armed guard who rode "shotgun" at the back of our 4x4 and slept outside our door at night. I guess you could say they comforted us!

I'm often asked, "If there is a God, why do terrible things happen in the world?" I ask, do we think that God is unilaterally responsible for the wellbeing of all people? – many of whom deny His existence or are totally ignoring Him, choosing instead to follow something or someone else? A tough question which we will come back to later.

When someone has entered into a shepherding relationship, however, it is a totally different story. A contract (otherwise known as a covenant) has been entered into that God will honour. David was able to say, "*I have made the Lord my refuge.*" What that means is, once a person has put his/her trust in God, He makes it His responsibility to look after and intervene in that person's life. The shepherding relationship has begun. Knowing this gives us amazing comfort. None of us really know what the next day will hold for us, let alone the next year of our life, but He knows. Shouldn't we, instead, trust that the Great Shepherd who is leading us has our wellbeing in hand? Whenever He needs to, He will step right on into our lives. Sometimes He has been known to do it through angelic intervention, and sometimes through the help of others – but He will always come to our aid.

Once, early on in our married life when Sue and I had just one son, we went on a holiday to the Mediterranean. He was not yet three years of age and not long after arriving at our apartment, unknown to us, he opened the door, let himself out and disappeared. We were staying at the top of a hill at the bottom of which was a deep harbour. We knew no one in the area – we'd literally just arrived! Once we realised he was gone we were greatly alarmed. We rushed out into the now almost darkness desperately, frantically searching. We were unknown in this town and knew no one. But then, a man appeared from around the corner with Joshua in his hands. He brought him right up to us and handed him over. We bent down to speak to our son, asking him, "Where have you been? Are you Ok?" and as we stood back up the man was gone, nowhere to be seen. We never saw him again. We think he was an angel.

I have known God intervene in many areas of life, helping to resolve crimes that the Police say are unsolvable and the BBC come and make a programme about it. He has intervened in travel arrangements and in the selling of property in an impossible economic climate. I have known God intervene in making introductions to people I've needed to meet, but who were impossible to reach. I have also known God rescue me from life-threatening situations. I *know* God intervenes! (You should See Sue's book *Is God There? You bet!* It's full of such stories).

Jesus Himself took on the mantle of the Great Shepherd. Read how He defined His relationship with His followers in John chapter 10. It is an amazing picture!

If you have ever seen a picture of an old-fashioned sheepfold, you may have noticed its unusual design – four stone walls, but no door. It had no door because at night, having ushered all the sheep into the fold, the shepherd himself would lie in the doorway. The only way to get in was to go through the shepherd – he literally was the door. What Jesus is telling us through this is: "No one can get at you because I am your Shepherd!"

A shepherd is there for the tough times

I write this in the middle of an economic recession, perhaps one of the worst the world has ever seen. During this year, many businesses in the nation, and therefore many people, are going through huge financial crises. During a time of such uncertainty and stress we really need a shepherd whose voice can lead and guide us, someone whose voice we can tune into who will steer us away from the cliff edges and precipices.

There have been times in my life when I have felt like giving up and quitting on my faith, but because God is my Shepherd and not my mentor, my shepherd and not simply my leader, my shepherd and not just my teacher … He came looking for me in those moments and picked me up. He wouldn't let me quit.

All of us have a constantly nagging voice in the back of our heads telling us we are not worthy or worth it. Some bloody minded people work harder to prove this voice wrong, but others just sink under low self-esteem. This shepherding relationship works even when we know the voice is right, we don't deserve it, but we get it anyway! WOW!

Occasionally, a shepherd couldn't be there for his sheep because he would need to attend to some other business. Then a hired hand would come and watch the sheep temporarily. If a lion or a bear showed up, however, the hired hand was likely to run. He would not risk his life defending the sheep because they were not his own. Jesus, however, said "*I am the good shepherd of the sheep. The good shepherd lays down his life for the sheep*" (John 10:11).

Some of us have entrusted our lives to "hired hand" leaders who disappeared the moment we needed them the most. But this Shepherd is willing to lay down his life, to go through thick and thin, whatever it takes. He's not a fair-weather friend; He's not there only for the good times. David was able to say, *"The Lord is my shepherd"* because he knew that whatever life threw at him, he had a Shepherd who would never, ever, leave him.

This Shepherd takes His responsibility seriously! No matter what you do, the bottom line is, *you have a Shepherd who is never going to leave you.*

> *"A drop of God's grace is worth an ocean of man's favour."*
>
> — *Derek Bingham*

2 *Where is My Life Going?*

IIIIIIIIIIIIIIIIIIIIIIIIIIIIIIIIIIIIIIIIIIIIIIIIIIIIIIIIIIIIIIIIIIIIIIIIIIIIIIIIIIIIIIIIIIIIIIIIIIIIIIIIIIIIIIIII

*"He makes me to lie down in green pastures;
He leads me beside the still waters."*

Is the life you've got the one you want? Ask yourself these questions:

◊ Is my life too busy?
◊ Do I consider myself to be stressed?
◊ Am I always in a hurry?
◊ Do I no longer feel I can give proper time to people?
◊ Do I constantly interrupt people, even before they have finished speaking?
◊ Do I use my day off to catch up on unfinished work?
◊ Does my life seem to lurch from one crisis to another?

These are tough questions to consider, aren't they? But this Psalm speaks into real situations, real issues, real problems. *"He makes me to lie down in green pastures; He leads me beside the still waters,"* speaks of a satisfied, purposeful, well-paced and enjoyable life. Is this the kind of life you long for?

The Shepherd's health check

One person said this: "The trouble with my life is that it's in tune with chaos." We all know people like this, don't we? Every time we meet them they, or someone in their family, have just fallen into another crisis! I think we could call it "white-water rafting". It's something you might do occasionally, but I don't think any of us would want to live like that all the time!

How is your chaos management? Does it look like this ...?

◊ Do you feel guilty when you sit down to relax?

◊ Is your "to-do" list longer than ever?

◊ Do you have to be ill before you get some rest?

◊ Do you fall asleep every time you sit down to relax?

◊ Are you too busy to get any time to reflect, meditate or get time with God?

◊ When did you last hear God say something to you so clearly you were able to tell others and repeat it?

◊ Do you have space in your life to learn something new or simply just be creative?

◊ Would you consider your life to be productive or simply very busy?

◊ Are you active but not really satisfied?

◊ Is there an emptiness deep inside you, a longing for something else, but you haven't found it yet?

All of these questions can be summed up in the question: *is the life you've got the one you really want?*

The Shepherd's good life

Maybe you struggled with some of those questions because of what you are going through at the moment? It is helpful to remind ourselves, however we feel, that the life God plans for us is meant to be *good* and enjoyable, and as John 10:10 says, *"lived to the full"*.

Maybe you are like some friends of mine, working hard to pay for the house they bought, the house of their dreams, but in order to get it, they're never in it! The work they do takes them away from home. Are we like them, giving our lives for something we can't even enjoy? I know a man who his whole life wanted a Porsche. He was successful and through a one-off bonus bought a black Carrera with red leather seats. It looked amazing. He parked it outside his house and would look at it every now and again through the window. Every so often he would jump to his feet, thinking he heard someone outside, or if a car alarm went off in the street he would jump up to check to see if it was his. In fact, he started a nightly routine of checking and double checking the car, making sure it was safe. He found himself sleeping restlessly, waking early, disturbed at the slightest of noises. One early morning, exhausted from lack of sleep, he took a blanket and curled up uncomfortably in the car itself, waiting until it was time to go to work. The week that followed saw a nightly routine of car sleeping! With no room at his house to build a garage, he began to look for other properties away from his area that had a place where he could keep his car safe. His partner, however, who didn't want to move and was tired of the distraction, promptly left him. Then the final blow came: he came out of work one day and his car had been stolen and was never recovered. The insurance company paid up and suddenly he had the money to buy another one. But did he? What would you do?

How many of us have sleepless or light sleep nights? Maybe not over Porsches, but due to work/money/exams or a thousand other areas?

Is the life we've got the one we want?

Fighting wars, subduing enemies, ruling a nation and raising a family must have kept king David pretty busy, never mind all the times he was on the run as a fugitive. Yet in and around his life was this constant, undergirding sense of deep, inner security and acceptance.

My friend got his Porsche and so wanted it to add to his identity and self esteem. For David, not one of his palaces, crowns or accolades added to his identity; he found security and comfort from being in a right relationship with his Shepherd. In fact, David attributed every good thing he had to the overflow of this relationship.

Many people look forward all year to their holiday and see this as the answer to their stressed out life, thinking it will make them restful and happy. But this is not the answer, because wherever you go, you're there! When David writes about the Shepherd leading us besides quiet, still waters, he is speaking more about inner conditions than outward circumstances.

While David was great, he was far from perfect. We shouldn't really mention his affair with his best mate's wife or the murder that followed. How could he live with himself? How can he claim to be living in this still waters zone? Shouldn't he be seeing a counsellor? Or at least taking tablets? But David learned something some Christians never get: God meets us on the platform of grace, not the platform of performance. He discovered that when he truly encountered God, He didn't raise his issues, He only confirmed his acceptance.

Part of looking ahead involves having goals. Some of us groan inwardly at the thought of setting targets for ourselves!

But God wants us to enjoy the journey to those goals too. He wants us to live every day being able to say, (like He did at the time of Creation) "This is good!" But how do we get from being stressed out, too busy, and not really enjoying life (and all too often being unhappy with ourselves) to a place where we can say life is good?

Every time we turn on the news and read the newspapers what we see is pressure, anxiety and worry. But the Bible says that when the Lord is Our Shepherd, we can go forward into the future with purpose and confidence where the road ahead looks very different. Psalms like Psalm 23 contain some hidden keys to making that change in our attitude.

The Shepherd's songs

Did you realise that all 150 psalms were songs written to music? Many of them were meant to be sung by choirs, but several of them were for private devotions. David was a singer and a worshipper, but there is no doubt that he was also the most macho of men. Remember that this guy took out the giant Goliath as a young lad! David loved nothing more than a good fight. When he heard the Philistines were coming, his response was, "Great!" Yet, it seemed as if he spent half his time singing. It was a way of life for him.

We had lunch with a friend recently who works in a nursing home for people who suffer severely from Alzheimer's and dementia. She shared that while these people often cannot remember who or where they are, they can often sing entire passages of Scripture, hymns or things they learnt as children. Somehow the music has latched itself to the memory and not been forgotten.

Songs have real power. They are the weapon of choice for some of the greatest Bible heroes. This was true of Moses, whose hymns are recorded, and some of the psalms were written by him. It was true of Miriam. It was true of Jesus. It was true of Peter. It was true of Paul and many others in the Scriptures. Is it true of you?

I believe that the Book of Psalms is there partly to teach you and me how to master this power of sung truth for ourselves. You may not be musical at all. You may even be embarrassed at your own tone (but you probably do still sing in the shower!) For most of us though, however well we sing, when stress, pressure and anxiety get a hold of our lives, the singing tends to stop. God wants it to be the other way around. If we can declare and speak out the truths contained in these Psalms, it could quite literally change the whole course of the day for us. Because we don't always know what to say, we're given 150 amazing songs of truth that we can choose from, that we can read, quote, memorise and learn, and speak into our own situations.

Just look at Psalm 103 and the sequence it takes-

Bless the LORD, O my soul,
and forget not all his benefits;
*Who forgives **all** your iniquities;*
Who heals all your diseases,
Who redeems your life from destruction
Who crowns you with lovingkindness and tender mercies
Who satisfies your mouth with good things
So that your youth is renewed like the eagle's.

When you know God forgives all your iniquities, past/present/future; when you know God is for you not against you, when you know this awesome Shepherd is approving you all day long – not because of your past performance, but your present standing – what a difference that makes! We asked in chapter one, what are some of the terms and conditions for this kind of shepherding relationship with God? One is this: decide today that you will never, ever, be able to perform well enough to have peace with God or peace with yourself! In other words, come to God in a different way – the way of grace. He made this way through Jesus, who God sees as perfect, and so when you place your life in Him, you're seen as He is! Not once, not twice, not when you perform well, but all the time. Even when you know you have messed up.

Some people think God's job is to tell you you're wrong and you need to change and do better, just like a school teacher. But the converse is the truth: God affirms by the Holy Spirit that your sins are forgiven and as we read above, all other things flow from this. You can be so still and at peace knowing this great Shepherd is for you.

> *"His Spirit bears witness with our spirit that we are children of God."*
>
> (Romans 8:16)

We need to get singing! And with the right words!

The Shepherd's security

I often watch international rugby. When the All Blacks do that threatening "war dance" before the game (the Haka), putting fear into people before a ball is even kicked or thrown, I am reminded that society can do the same to us. We live in a world that is constantly trying to preoccupy us and fill our minds with fear, concern and stress.

But the Psalms are there to challenge what is thrown at us, so that the horizon of our minds is filled, not with the fear of the moment, but with the greatness of our God. If, even in the worst possible situations, we dwell on the magnitude of

God, AND how much He is favourable towards us, this will elevate us with a secure hope for the day ahead.

This I know, my God is for me!

(see Romans 8:31)

The phrase *"He makes me lie down"* is one used particularly of animals that are made to feel secure. At its root is the concept of being safe, accepted and at rest. Many of us are living a life that ends up in strife, simply because we are not secure. We constantly feel we're having to prove ourselves.

Maybe when you were a child comments were made that you weren't as clever as your sister or brother? Or maybe you were told that if you worked really hard and put the effort in, you could make your life count and go somewhere? So now you're trying to prove something. Some of us think that acceptance comes by wearing the right badges, driving the right cars or living at the right addresses. But in James 1:18 (NCV) the Bible says this:

"God decided to give us life through the word of truth so we might be the most important of all the things he made."

Your security is never going to be found in anything you achieve or anything you've gained. It's going to be found in the fact that you are accepted by the God who loved and made you.

Randolph Hearst, a wealthy publisher, decided that he would spend his billions collecting rare treasures. One day he opened a magazine to find a beautiful artefact, so he hired a man to go and find it for him, wherever it was in the world. He received a telegram a little while later from the man saying, "I've got good news and more good news for you. The good news is that I've found the artefact and I know where it is. But the better news is that it's in your warehouse. You already own it!" One wise man wrote, "Happy is the man who wants what he's already got." Mr Hearst had so many possessions that he didn't know what he possessed! Every day he was getting up and simply wanting more.

Sometimes we can fall into the trap of caring about who we are connected with or being in the right circles, thinking these things will somehow add to our importance. But when you come to a place of security that God is for you, those things don't seem to matter. He's making you lie down, not stand up and look important. I am completely secure that God is for me. Are you?

The Shepherd's food

David was able to say, *"He makes me lie down in green pastures and he leads me beside quiet waters."* We all know that sheep need green pasture on which to feed. But not everything that calls itself "food" is good for us. Not everything is God's "green pasture". Do you remember a story in the press some time ago about fake baby food in China? Some of the world's biggest manufacturers of infant food were, for cost reasons, manufacturing in China. Now, the Chinese, being very good at copying, decided to mimic the baby food. But their food was in fact not nutritious at all. In reality, it was actually harmful to children!

According to reports from both the BBC and Chinese national newspapers, dozens of babies were treated for malnutrition in two Chinese provinces after babies were given fake infant formula by their unwitting parents. After being given these formulas the affected babies lost weight rapidly. Thousands of babies either died or were seriously affected. The parents were feeding this so-called baby food to the babies, but they were losing weight and becoming weaker and weaker. Not everything we take in is good for us.

The human soul is made to be hungry. I'm not just talking about the physical body, but also the soul. It wants to "eat" and it wants to be satisfied. It has been created with an appetite. The appetite is meant to be fed by relationship with God. That's why God put the hunger there.

Somebody once said to me, "Why do you experience pain if there is a God?" My answer was simple: He gave us pain to keep us safe, so that when we put our hand in a fire we don't leave it there! God gave us those sensations for our good. In the same way, God gave us "soul hunger" in order that we go looking for and find Him. Isaiah says,

"Why spend your money on something that is not real food?
Why work for something that doesn't really satisfy you?
Listen closely to me, and you will eat what is good;
your soul will enjoy the rich food that satisfies."

(Isaiah 55:2 NCV)

When we rush around trying to feed ourselves on entertainment, on more acquisitions and on better education, none of these things are ever going to satisfy us the way that God can when He leads us into His green pastures.

In particular God's green pasture is called the "Gospel" or Good News. What is this good news? God has made it possible for me to be accepted and favourable to Him without me doing one thing! It's called grace. And as you come and hear it or read it, it's just like eating excellent food.

The Shepherd's leading

The Shepherd leads us beside still, not rushing waters. Our lives are meant to be lived in peace. There are moments when worries come, but we are not meant to live in a place of stress all the time.

Some of us have gone "white-water rafting" because we haven't allowed the Shepherd to lead us at all. We don't submit our plans, our thoughts or our intentions to God, but make up our own and ask for them to be blessed. I've learnt as a pastor that it's better to say, "God, show me what you're blessing and let me move in on it," rather than saying, "Bless what I'm doing." That kind of lifestyle requires a deliberate act of allowing God to be ahead of us. We have to submit to the Shepherd's leading.

The Bible makes it clear that we've been created as a tripartite being. We have a body. The body is simply a suit. If I go out to space I need a spacesuit to live in that environment. If I live on earth I need an earth-suit: it's called a body. One day the body will die or the body will be changed, as the Bible says (1 Corinthians 15:51).

The real me lives inside this suit and it's got two components: a spirit and a soul. The spirit is the real me that's eternal. It's the part of me that receives life from God and is the part of me that God wants to connect with and lead. My soul is also God-given. It's my emotions, my mind and my will. Feelings stir in there. God gave me those feelings. I'm not only meant to know about God, but I'm meant to feel and sense Him.

I can be led by any one of these three parts of myself. My body has got a voice and appetites. Sometimes all it seems to say is, "Feed me! Feed me! Chocolate! Chocolate!" Isn't it awful when you discipline yourself all day and then at 8pm you think, "Oh, hang it …" and you've just undone all that you were trying to do? All that pain and all those times you've said no all day! But your body is a temple of God – His dwelling place (1 Corinthians 6:19). So it is possible to submit to His leading in every area of our body and its desires.

My soul has a voice too, often expressed in emotions. You can feel down, feel up, feel lonely and that is a kind of craving as well. Our mind plays a big part in this. Romans 12:2 teaches us that our minds can be renewed by God in order that we may "... *test and approve what God's will is—his good, pleasing and perfect will.*" This wonderful psalm teaches us that God wants to restore our very souls to make them what He wants them to be (v3).

The spirit also has a voice which I liken to the conscience, and that too needs to be inspired by the voice of God. We are taught that God Himself is Spirit and that we must worship Him in Spirit and in truth (see John 4:24). Galatians 4:6 tells us that because we are "... *sons, God sent the Spirit of his Son into our hearts, the Spirit who calls out, 'Abba, Father'.*" God communicates with us on a Spirit-to-spirit basis.

To be led in this way with our body, soul and spirit means that we have to let God be in control. So how does the Good Shepherd seek to lead us?

The Shepherd's guidance

I often speak about the 5 C's of how God speaks to and guides us:

• *Confirmation of His Word*
How do I know God is leading me into something? His Word, the Bible, will always confirm the action that I'm about to take. He will also often confirm through this word the actions He wants me to take.

• *Conviction in my spirit*

Have you ever had a conviction, a growing sense of what you need to do? God speaks to our spirits and we begin to apprehend it and pick it up. What was the promise that Jesus said we would receive in Acts 1:4? It was the Holy Spirit. God speaks to me in my spirit and I get a conviction. I got such a conviction to move to Scotland nearly 20 years ago. It started as a deep sense that this was what God was saying to me. All great journeys seem to begin with a conviction. You need to pay attention to the convictions that start in your spirit. When you tune in and listen well, those convictions can begin to speak to you and guide you.

• *Counsel of shepherds*

In Jeremiah 3:15 (NKJV) God says this, *"And I will give you shepherds according to My heart."* Not only did Jesus say He was the Great Shepherd, but He turned to Peter at the breakfast on the beach and said, *"Feed my sheep"* (John 21:17). God wants His people led well and so the council of shepherds, people who are serving and seeking God, are who He designs to help lead us. These people, according to Hebrews 13:17, will have to give an account for the souls they are shepherding and leading. Relationships with such people count. We'd be foolish to take a major judgement, decision or change of direction without the counsel of wise shepherds in our lives.

• *Calling forwards*

Is the action or the course I'm about to take going to call me forward to become more like Jesus? That is what the Holy Spirit's role is in my life: to conform me to the image of God's Son. I have to ask at all times, "Is this going to help me to become more like Jesus and advance the cause of His kingdom?"

• *Complete peace*

When all these things come together we are left with a deep inner peace. Even if the circumstances are not favourable or things haven't changed on the outside, "... *the peace of Christ guards our hearts*" (Philippians 4:7). This word in Greek means to act as an umpire, to say, "That's out, that's in, that's okay ..." It leaves us with a deposit of peace when we know and understand God's will for us.

God does not want us to live a life of pure struggle and strife. That is what the world is like. God says, "Come out of it ... let me lead you beside stiller waters."

Life with Him is different. There are lots of goals I want to achieve in my future and there are many exciting things I want to see happen. Many of these goals will take a lot of effort to achieve. But the bottom line is this: I am hopeful and expectant. I believe that God wants me to live in peace, rest, abundance, and great provision. No wonder David is able to say, (when) "the Lord's my shepherd I shall not want." The road ahead is going to be a good one because we are following a good Shepherd.

> *"God's grace puts into us what God wants*
> *out of us".*
>
> —*Roy Hession*

3 *Finding True Restoration*

IIIIIIIIIIIIIIIIIIIIIIIIIIIIIIIIIIIIIIIIIIIIIIIIIIIIIIIIIIIIIIIIIIIIIIIIIIIIIIIIIIIIIIIIIIIIIIIIIIIIIIIIIIIIIIIIIIIIIIIIIIII

"He restores my soul; He leads me in the paths of righteousness For His name's sake."

(Psalm 23:3)

The People's Psalm

Psalm 23 is the most quoted part of the Bible. Just look at where it has turned up:

Songs as diverse as Coolio's *Gangsta's Paradise* and Marilyn Manson's In the *Shadow of the Valley of Death* from the album *Holy Wood*; films such as *Pulp Fiction*, *Sister Act* and TV programmes such as *The Vicar of Dibley* all contain references to David's song.

Various people, such as George W. Bush, have used quotes from Psalm 23 in speeches of significance in recent history. Patti Smith, the American singer, artist and poet, has also sought inspiration from these words. It has apparently been used in more than 150 movies, pop songs or novels.

So it appears to be a psalm that people can relate to readily. But I wonder how many of them really, truly understand it?

The Shepherd's restoration

*Now we come to the verse: "He restores my soul;
He leads me in the paths of righteousness For His
name's sake. "*

(Psalm 23:3)

I think it is highly significant that the Bible explains the truth
that God *heals* our body but *restores* our soul. It's popular
these days to talk about the "healing of our emotions".
There are certainly many books available on the subject.
Titles such as *Healing for Damaged Emotions* are freely
available. But we *never* find that phrase in Scripture. What
we do discover is this: God ministers health to our bodies
but brings restoration to our souls. Everyday our souls are
exposed to soul damage. When our souls get damaged *we
lose the ability to believe, conceive and receive!*

Maybe even as you are reading this you are suffering
from a suffocating depression that is weighing you down?
Or maybe immense discouragement or deep disappointment
is troubling you? Others now find that their every approach
to any good or positive thing is deep scepticism, or the worst
of wit-synicism, yet I believe that God wants to set you free
from it today. In His Word there is true comfort and hope, so
listen carefully to what He wants for your soul.

We all face times of anxiety, discouragement and hurt. Life,
and the circumstances we find ourselves in, can damage us
badly. To say God *restores* our soul, speaks of a real process.
It's not often about "instant emotional healing" as some
secular books promise. Restoration is a key biblical theme
that simply means: to bring back again, to turn things around
and to recompense. It's not just about putting something
back, *but it's about putting it back better than it was before.*

The good Shepherd does not just restore us by mending us, He makes us new!

The Shepherd's intention

The good Shepherd doesn't only want to restore the Church to its original *condition* (like the early New Testament Church), He wants to restore it to its original *intention*. His intention is that His Church is powerful and significant, that its voice carries and the work it engages in communicates life and changes cities. The same is true of us and our souls. God doesn't just want to put us in a place where He "gets us through life". He wants to restore our lives not to their original condition, but to His original *intention*, where we are finally living life to the full.

It's perfectly possible to have a good job, enough money, a comfortable home and yet still be totally miserable, isn't it? You may have gone through a divorce or may have serious problems in your marriage. Perhaps there are worries with your children or there may be deep issues eating away at your self-esteem? All of these things can rob you of life. So, when Jesus said, "*I have come to give you life*" (John 10:10) He was talking about the restoration of your soul, so that you are in a position to *really* live and to enjoy the life that He gives you.

So, biblical restoration is about our Shepherd bringing us back again, turning things around and making us new in the very depths of our soul. It is no accident that the Apostle John wrote in the New Testament:

> "*Beloved, I pray that in all respects you may prosper and be in good health, just as your **soul prospers**.*"
>
> (3 John 1:2 NASB)

Or, I could paraphrase it in this way:

"Your whole life, in every detail, will prosper in direct relation to how your soul prospers."

The degree to which your soul thrives will impact the degree to which your life flourishes. The good Shepherd is working away in my soul to restore it to the place of life, wholeness and wellbeing He desires. The result of this is that, "I shall not want. I shall lack nothing." Isn't it great to know that God is concerned about every detail?

I want to show you a few very important areas in which God restores our souls:

The Shepherd restores us from guilt

One of my boys came home from school one day and said to his brother, "Is Mum in?"

"No, she's still at work," came the reply.

He then went to his bedroom, sat on his bed and opened his Bible to read it.

Now, you might think, "What a good, spiritual little boy!" Shall I tell you what I thought? My first reaction was, "What has he done? That's the action of someone who's feeling guilty about something!" Every one of us, outside of Christ, has good reason to feel guilty. Guilt is a killer. In Psalm 38, David writes, *"My guilt has overwhelmed me like a burden too heavy to bear"* (Psalm 38:4 NIV).

One man speaking about life said this:

"Every man has his public life, his private life and his secret life."

We don't often worry about guilt in our public life or even our private life, unless something about us has been exposed. But what about our secret lives? It's true that we all have plenty to feel guilty about. None of us are perfect and we can't hide our sin from God.

Sometimes we can try to deny it or ignore it, but guilt is a heavy burden to bear. We can minimize it and say it doesn't matter. Or we can compromise. We can simply say, "Well, everybody's doing it, I'm no worse." We can rationalise it and try to explain it away. When we carry guilt in our hearts, not only can we sometimes try and justify it, but we can also try and shift the blame to others or to other things: "Well, I did that because when I was young I was left alone ... I wasn't potty trained properly ... I didn't get the support that I needed ... people were not there for me, so that's why I went out and robbed a bank!"

When we lived in West Yorkshire, I enjoyed working in the local maximum security prison. Most people there were serving life sentences for serious crimes such as multiple rapes, murder or armed robbery. This last couple of years we've been working in Kilmarnock Prison. The first thing many inmates tell me is: "I'm not guilty ... I didn't do it ... it's not my fault." Or, and this is a huge sector of the prison population, "I killed a man, I just don't remember doing it. I was stoned at the time." In split seconds whole lives are lost.

We may have been brought up by well-meaning parents and given relatively good opportunities in life, so it's possible that we didn't fall to that degree, but guilt comes in all kinds of shapes and sizes: "I wasn't the mother that I should have been ... I wasn't there for my wife when she needed me ... I didn't handle the money properly ... I should have worked harder at school ... I shouldn't have had that affair..." etc.

The Shepherd restores us from shame

When guilt is eating away at our lives a number of things can happen:

We can beat ourselves up over it. Day in, day out, we run the footage of our failure in our heads. One thing is for sure: when guilt is resident, faith has no room to operate. We need faith to live as God intended. John wrote, *"This is the victory that has overcome the world, even our faith"* (1 John 5:4 NIV). Faith like this leans on the good Shepherd and trusts His Word to restore our souls. Sometimes the moment you articulate that kind of faith, it's squashed by feelings of guilt, self-blame and shame. "Why would God do anything for me when I've still got a problem in this area? How can I ask for His hand in my life when I did this to that person?" Maybe you have felt the power of the re-runs of such footage in your own life? Such guilt has a habit of not only projecting us back into the past in a negative way, it also robs us of our present and threatens our future.

But the good Shepherd restores and takes us out of our guilt. This is why the Gospel of Jesus is so unique and so amazing. I've examined many other religions and heard what people believe and why. Not one of those religions or one of those people has an answer for guilt outside of the cross. None of them do! All other religions tell you, whichever one you care to look at, that you must work harder and try to *do better.* You have to work at improving your life, try to be kind, try to be merciful and try to be peaceful. But what about the guilt we already feel? What about the shame that's in our hearts? What about the things that are weighing us down? What about the self-blame that derails our faith when we need God's presence and power in our lives?

Paul was right when he said, *"For I am not ashamed of the gospel of Christ, for it is the power of God to salvation for everyone who believes,"* (Romans 1:16 NKJV). Then he wrote to the Colossians and said this:

"Having cancelled out the certificate of debt consisting
of decrees against us, which was hostile to us; and He
has taken it out of the way, having nailed it to the cross."
(Colossians 2:14 NASB)

So, we *are* wrong. We *are* sinful, but the Bible says *He*
has cancelled out all evidence against us and has taken our
guilt and nailed it to the cross! What good news we have
to share!

You will probably know that your body contains organs
that purify the blood – a liver and two kidneys. When they
function properly, they take the rubbish from your system,
out of the blood supply, so that your body can work as it
was intended to. Our good Shepherd, Jesus, is just like this.
When He hung on the cross, every sense of blemish, guilt
and stain I deserve to feel was transformed into something
holy, amazing, acceptable and changed.

The Shepherd we follow restores our souls from guilt
releasing us from the pressures of shame. A story is told of
the man of faith, Martin Luther. As the power of the Gospel
was being revealed to him and he began to understand that
he was saved by grace, through faith (and not by penances
or going up the Vatican steps or by Hail Mary's and religious
artefacts) he was sitting in his study and the devil came to
him. Satan began to list all the sins in Luther's life. As he
listened, Luther wrote them down with his quill on a piece
of paper. When the devil had run out of things to say, Luther
wrote across the top of it all, "Paid in Full by the Blood of
Jesus." It is said that he then picked up his inkwell and threw
it at the devil, hitting the wall, shouting, "Get out of here!
I'm free in Jesus' name!" He had understood the power of
the good Shepherd to restore. Isn't that awesome?

You may say to me, "Andrew, you don't know what
I've done. I don't deserve that kind of restoration." Before

becoming an Apostle, the Bible tells us in Acts 8 that Paul (then known as Saul) gave approval to Stephen's death. He murdered many other Christians. And yet he writes with such confidence later in 1 Timothy 1:15, *"Here is a faithful saying and worthy of all acceptance, that Christ Jesus came into the world to save sinners—of whom I am the chief."* Paul knew he was both saved and free.

Many people find themselves unhappier after coming to Christ than before, since the voice of condemnation is so loud inside them. They forever feel like God does not accept them and is turning His back on them every time they sin. BUT THAT ISN'T TRUE! God affirms them and confirms them. The Holy Spirit restores our souls by reminding us God is for us; He has accepted us and continues to accept us, not due to anything we have done, but by what *He* has done – that's why we call it grace.

"Let us draw near with a true heart in full assurance of faith, having our hearts sprinkled from an evil conscience."

(Hebrews 10:22)

The Shepherd restores us from failure

God accepts us and loves us in spite of our failures. It's that simple. We were once away preaching and gave an opportunity for prayer at the end. A man came forward who was completely distraught, unable to shake off his guilt. He was a Christian, but the shame and failure he felt had meant that his life had been frozen in time for many years. He'd walked for several years in depression and sadness. After the meeting, he came forward in floods of tears because he'd been hearing about forgiveness.

"There is no answer for what I've done," he said. But one of the pastors asked, "What is it that you've done that you think is so awful?" He said, "Well, I'm a farmer. One day I'd been out with my shotgun and I came home. Because I was in a hurry I propped it up against the back door whilst it was still loaded. My eleven year-old son picked it up and by accident shot himself dead. It was my fault."

With a revelation of wisdom the pastor said to him, "God the Father knew what it was to kill His own Son, *on purpose*. He fully understands what you feel. God wants you to know today that no matter what you've done, there is a release and a restoring." In a second that man's demeanour and life was transformed and he was set free to continue to pick up his walk with God again.

However you feel today and whatever thoughts of guilt, shame or failure have dogged your life, the good Shepherd wants you to know His power to completely restore you. Perhaps you need restoration in your work or your family, your health or in your relationships? Remember afresh today His desire and promise to restore *your* soul. There is nothing the enemy can do to stop you going forward, because everything is already done. It's built and based on the love of God. And there is nothing we can be more sure of, in this world, or the next.

> *"For I am persuaded that neither death nor life, nor angels nor principalities nor powers nor things present nor things to come; nor height nor depth, nor any other created thing, shall be able to separate us from the love of God which is in Christ Jesus our LORD."*
>
> (Romans 8:38-39)

The Shepherd restores us to strength

The good Shepherd does not just restore us *away* from guilt, shame and failure. He chooses to restore us *towards* new strength. He delivers us from one state into another.

On our own we are weak, but in Him we are strong! Have you lost the ability to be expectant and to conceive a dream in faith? Have circumstances robbed you of your confidence in a God who hears and answers prayer?

Amongst the list of faith-filled Bible heroes in Hebrews is Sarah (See Hebrews 11:11). Sarah may have been old, barren and past child-bearing age, but she was given the ability and strength to conceive. In this she was fully restored.

You and I need to perceive what God's plans are for us too. We need to be able to glimpse a part of the future. You and I were called for a life of significance. But when our souls have been damaged by discouragement, disappointments, disillusionment and depression, it's very difficult to conceive that anything else can come our way. We start to settle into a, "Let's just get through another day" kind of existence.

When the Shepherd restores us to strength, however, He brings us back to the place where not only are we guilt-free, but where we can function fully. There's a vibrancy of new life inside us. We can begin to look forward to the year that is to come.

The Shepherd restores our emotional strength

Some of us don't know how to handle our emotions at all. We try to kill them dead or ignore them, or we live completely ruled by them. But God gives us our emotions for a reason. When we start to feel an emotional response to something, we must come back to the Bible, make the

Lord our Shepherd all over again and let Him take us on the journey towards restoration.

Have you ever made a relatively harmless comment to someone, only for them to "blow up" in your face, and the torrent of their anger was way out of proportion to the trigger that you'd given? Maybe you struggle with anger in your own life and even as you read this.

Sometimes the emotions we face are ones of fear or anxiety. Are you fearful, afraid to go out and afraid to come in? Some people are even afraid to go to church. One Sunday morning, a woman cried her way through my entire talk. I kept thinking, "What have I said?" When I spoke to her at the end, she explained, "These aren't tears of sadness, they're tears of joy. I've sat in this meeting today and it's the first time in over nineteen years that I've been in a crowd and not felt such fearful anxiety that I've had to run out!" During the week, she had given her life to Jesus and she was already experiencing change. A restoration of her soul was happening. The good Shepherd was restoring her to strength.

It's possible that you're living in a world of excessive anger, fear, anxiety or depression because of a physical condition. There may be a chemical or hormonal imbalance in your mind or body. Maybe you are battling with a disease? It's also possible that if you've lived a life of drug-taking, even soft drugs, it has affected your wellbeing in some way. If you've been and checked that out, or looked at that and it is confirmed, remember that God heals sick bodies and sick minds.

But sometimes the cause is altogether different. It can be physical changes that we struggle to handle – especially women at a certain point in the month or at the age when that point of change comes. I know guys like cracking jokes about this, but it can be a real issue for women and a real issue for the men in the marriage! Let me tell you something else: sometimes the hormonal changes that a woman goes through at a certain point in her life can completely wreck whole families. I have a friend who is a seasoned minister, a well-known name in the Christian world. He and his wife spend a considerable amount of time ministering to other couples who struggle with this very issue. He said, "Christian couples who've been married twenty-five, even thirty-five years, are deciding to divorce. They've raised the children, they've got through financial hardship and gone through so much together. Everything should start to become easier but, instead, their relationship begins to fall apart."

He explained that often, when a woman hits a certain point of hormonal and emotional imbalance and change, the results are so drastic that the couple don't know how to deal with it. The challenge is that one day the marriage can be perfectly normal and the next day it can be totally different. This is what he said to me, "I have heard this phrase from so many men: 'This is not the woman I married. I don't recognise this person.'" Then he said of himself, "We nearly lost our marriage when we went through the same thing."

I haven't found any books or teaching series on this issue yet! But the truth still holds: He can and will restore our souls, whatever the reason or whatever the season.

The Shepherd restores our goals

We can often get confused between godly goals and godly desires if we get godly goals and godly desires mixed up.

Let's say there is a lady. The lady is married and has children. She has a desire. The desire is for a happy, harmonious, godly "getting along well" family where every one of her kids behaves as they should. Is it conceivable for a Christian woman to have such a desire? Of course. Would you say it's a godly desire? It is.

However, if she turns that desire into her *goal,* what is the likely result? Because her goal is unachievable, in that it depends on so many factors, she may not see any progress. She will then feel disappointment and frustration. Children go through seasons too. They hit the terrible twos or the teenage years, or they get involved in unhealthy relationships. We need to be careful not to set ourselves goals that are completely beyond our control or we may end up saying, "It's my fault as a mother, my fault as a wife. My family should be a perfect Christian family by now. My children should all be saved and serving God in Africa somewhere. They shouldn't be smoking dope and smelling like they haven't washed for weeks. It's all my fault."

You can't control how your husband acts; you can't legislate for how your children behave; you can't organise everything that goes on in your life! If you confuse a desire with a goal, you may be setting yourself up to fail. When you do this, you're going to one of take two roads. Firstly, you may try and manipulate the situation and strive to make it right. So, you try to sort out your husband's problems by putting verses in his lunchbox or turning on the God channel. You try to get your son saved by inviting the pastor round for tea and you put a Bible on the table for him to read. You try to manipulate things.

Or, secondly you try to pressurise the people involved. You say to your children: "You should read your Bible ... here I've bought you a Christian CD." You start trying to control your world because you've made what should stay a godly desire into an unachievable goal. We men can do this with careers and jobs and all kinds of things if we are not careful.

If your goal is blocked time and time again, do you know what's going to happen? You are going to become very angry. I often talk to men and say this: you want to provide for your family, you seek to give them a good home, food on the table and a comfortable lifestyle. Is that a good desire? Yes. But if your *goal* is to do this and you see yourself hitting your forties and your ideal is slipping away from you, you can become very angry. You see your boss, the children or somebody else, as standing in your way. Therefore, it doesn't take much – an odd conversation or comment – for you to "blow up", because underneath you're suffering from "blocked goal syndrome".

Sometimes we're fearful and anxious because we don't even know what our goals are. We don't know what we want or how to get there. So because you have a desire and don't know how to achieve it, whatever happens it's all wrong. You end up constantly living in a world of anxiety and fear.

The Shepherd helps us achieve our goals

But if our desires are turned into godly goals, they are highly achievable. Jesus said this: *"Seek first His kingdom and His righteousness"* (Matthew 6:33). Notice how Psalm 23 ties these things together: *"He restores my soul"* is followed by *"He guides me in paths of righteousness."* They are connected. If our desires become godly goals after seeking first the Shepherd and His righteousness, then the woman we spoke of earlier might say this: "I realise that I can't fix my family. Even if I fast and pray for forty days, I can't change them. But I will love and accept them for who they are. I will be the best wife and mother that I can be, in the strength of the Shepherd who leads me."

This kind of goal is in your grasp because it only affects you. It stops you passing blame, stops you passing judgement and stops you projecting your failure onto others. It is a good goal. It's *your* goal!

When that goal is working away in your life by faith, you change. God always takes us on a journey, not of gaining things but of changing. What goals does the good Shepherd have for your life? Maybe they are as simple as, "How can I show my husband more respect? How can I take more of an interest in my children?" When we allow the good Shepherd to set our goals, we are going to see success because He will be at work in us, leading the way.

When we allow the good Shepherd to shape our goals we are brought back into line. The outcome is that we are able to start walking in a new direction with new purpose. We become characterised by success and not failure. God not only restores our goals *but He helps us achieve them*!

I have a desire to see our church, Destiny Glasgow, become 14,000 people. The week before we moved to Scotland, God spoke to me in a dream and I believe He gave me that number. Today, we've got dozens of churches and several thousand people involved. Is 14,000 people an achievable goal in my hands? I don't think it is.

I have to say that for years I *did* think it was, so I worked and toiled to make it happen. But every time I read my Bible it tells me this: one plants, one waters, but God gives the increase. So, what can I do towards this goal? Well, I can preach the Gospel more this year than in any other year before. I can train leaders, so that when people come into church they are loved and discipled well. That is achievable. I can do that with Christ's help. Those are goals in my hands. Goals like this are achieved with two clear outcomes. The belief that, "I didn't do this, it's God!" and the realisation that, "I am not striving and struggling to produce anything. This was always God's plan."

See how the good Shepherd restores your soul? He takes you on paths of righteousness walking by faith. I used to think "walking by faith" meant giving up your job, having no income and trusting God for your bus fare and the food on your table! I've been there and done that. And many Christians are called to walk like this. But for most of us, walking by faith simply means that we function in our daily lives on the basis of what we believe. What we believe determines our behaviour. After all, **we don't** *feel* **our way into good behaviour, we** *behave* **our way into good feelings**. Imagine that I set myself a goal that I'm going to become the best father I can be. I believe that the good Shepherd leads me onwards towards that goal and I will start to behave as a better father would.

The Shepherd restores His image in us

When we are fully restored in our souls we become more and more like Jesus. Just look at some of the things that God says about us as His sheep. I've put a few things together here, but I could have listed many more.

"*I am the salt of the earth*" (see Matthew 5:13). This tells us that we can flavour everyone and every situation around us. You don't need much salt in order to taste it, but you can tell if it is absent in a meal.

"*I am the light of the world*" (see Matthew 5:14). This means we bring hope and sunshine into people's lives. What do people think when you walk into the room? Do they murmur and move away? Or are the glad to see you? Do you make a difference to the atmosphere? Do you bring light into dark places?

"*I am a child of God*" (see John 1:12). I've loved raising my kids. One of the memories I have is of playing that little game where they would stand on a step and say, "Catch

me, Daddy!" then jump into my arms. Then they would
go two steps up, three steps up, and so on. I couldn't catch
them now! But the security and fun of knowing that we are
children of God is precious and priceless.

"I am a channel of Christ's life on earth" (see John 15:5).
We take the life from the good Shepherd and we bring it to
others. My wife is often more daring than me. Sometimes
when we go somewhere, she'll carry something with her –
maybe a CD or a book to give away. We were sitting on a
ferry crossing the Hudson River in New York and there was
a lady sitting in front of us. Sue tapped her on the shoulder
and said, "Excuse me, God's told me to give you this," and
gave her a CD. A conversation started up and we found out
that the woman was extremely wealthy. She had a niece who
was a Christian who had been talking to her for years about
knowing Jesus. We don't know how that story will end, but
we know that God could use us at any time to be His channel
of blessing to others.

"I am called by Jesus to bear a lot of fruit" (see John 15).
We are called to bear fruit and not just fruit that dies off, but
the kind that lasts. We can be full of expectant hope that we
will grow towards what we are reaching for because this is
the good Shepherd's goal for us.

"I am inclined to do right" (see Romans 6:18). Before you
become a Christian and the life of God is inside you, you're
inclined to do wrong, but this passage teaches us that once we
know and love Christ we become a "slave of righteousness."
God puts His Spirit inside you to enable you to do the right
thing. In fact, you have to fight it to do the wrong thing.

"I am joyfully enslaved to God" (see Romans 6:16). I
remember being at a dinner party in South Africa and
someone asked what I did for a living. I told them I worked
for the world's biggest employer. They said, "You work
for Wal-Mart? Microsoft? A bank?" I said, "No, I work for

the Church." I just love serving God because He's a great and wonderful Master. Did you know that God, my Boss and the One I work for, is the biggest employer on earth? 37 million people are serving God full-time. My Boss has mobilised the world's biggest voluntary workforce! They work for Him for nothing because they love Him so much. He's so great and it's a total joy and delight to serve Him. And we have an office in every city on Earth – how about that!

"I am a son of God. God is my Father" (see Romans 8:17). I am a co-heir with Christ. Everything that belongs to Him is now rightfully mine.

"I am a temple, a place, in which God dwells" (see 1 Corinthians 6:19). Our bodies are dwelling places of the Spirit of God. He lives within us and makes us His own.

"I am a new creation" (see 2 Corinthians 5:17). The old is gone and the new has come! It is no longer us that live but Christ that lives in us (Galatians 2:20).

"I am completely reconciled to and with God" (see 2 Corinthians 5:18). Me and God ... we're close! There's no problem in my relationship with Him. I sometimes do things wrong, but when God restores my soul from guilt it's not just an event, it's a whole condition. I have become the righteousness of God in Christ Jesus.

"I am a saint" (see Ephesians 1:4). Can you see my halo?! The devil wants you to think that you're a sinner, but the Bible says that you're a saint. Saint Andrew ... it's got a certain ring to it, don't you think?!

"I am God's handiwork" (see Ephesians 2:10). He made you and He made you as you are. He's still working to produce an amazing thing in your life. You are His workmanship.

"I am hidden with Christ in God" (see Colossians 3:3). Nothing can get at me! I'm safely hidden alongside Jesus in the very heart of the Father. What a place to belong!

"I am chosen specifically by God and dearly loved" (see Colossians 3:12). When I get up in the morning God's wanting to tell me, "I love you!" You and I are dearly loved by our heavenly Father.

"I am born of God and the devil can't touch me" (see 1 John 5:18). Jesus keeps us safe and the enemy has no hold over us.

When we know the truth of the good Shepherd's image in us, we are well on the road to true restoration. Dealing with our emotions, failures, doubts and fears is not a *power* encounter, it's a *truth* encounter. It's not what we feel or what we can do, it's what *He has done for us* that counts. Our good Shepherd restores our souls and He leads us forward *"in paths of righteousness for **His** name's sake."* When my soul is restored and my life is where God wants it to be, people look and say, "That's amazing!" His name gets the glory and the credit.

I want more of that.

Don't you?

4 "Proven Paths" of Righteousness

⅄⅄

*"He leads me in paths of righteousness for
His name's sake."*

(Psalm 23:3)

The need for the pathways

In my Bible, there is a little letter beside the word "paths" which gives the alternative word "tracks". So, we could read, "He guides me in 'tracks' of righteousness." Maybe you've walked up hills or mountains and picked out the narrow sheep tracks through the undergrowth? These little paths can often only be seen clearly when you are *right on top of them*, but they offer a way up – a way that is proven, trodden and tested by others that have gone before. I believe that David is talking here about God giving him specific ability to make specific choices about specific questions in life to follow those narrow, proven tracks laid out up the mountain.

Why does God provide us with such pathways? Why doesn't He let us make our own way up the mountain? I believe its part of who He is as our Shepherd. He gives us pathways:

1. To help us navigate our way through difficult terrain
2. To remind us that we are not alone; others have gone before us.
3. To make it easier for us to get through both the peaks and the pitfalls of life in a consistent way.
4. To help us climb the mountain to a higher level and give us a clearer view of our circumstances and of a vision of a preferred future.

I think that's a wonderful way to live! Don't you?

God wants us to live in such a way, and along such a path, that goodness and mercy follow us. Why do God's goodness and love track us like this? They know where to find us! We are on a well-trodden road. David is able to come to the point at the end of this psalm, where he is sure that God's goodness and mercy actively pursue him all the days of his life. Why is he so confident of this truth? I believe it is because he is travelling a well-trodden road that God has shown him.

Do you feel today as though you are wandering around on the mountain somewhere on your own? Or are you certain you are on the narrow track of God's provision? Do you need to take some time to rediscover some of the lessons learnt by those who have gone before you?

Even if I experience deep, dark valleys, His goodness and mercy will never stop pursuing me, even there. God says to me, "Andrew, stay on these pathways and they will bring you through to the place I have chosen for you." These pathways can be easily missed if we are not paying attention. Often, like sheep tracks, they are not very visible, hidden as they are by bracken and heather. But these slender paths are the way that the Shepherd leads us, empowering us to become who we are meant to be in Him.

The pathway to significance

At the turn of the 20th Century there was an asylum on the outskirts of Boston that dealt with severely mentally disturbed individuals. The staff tried everything they could to help a little girl called Annie who had been committed to the asylum. Yet, having tried all the treatments they could think of, they were without success. So little Annie was assigned to a padded prison cell in the basement of the asylum to live out her life.

A member of staff who worked there was a Christian lady. She wasn't a qualified medic, she was simply a carer who came in to do menial duties. But she had real compassion for Annie and decided that having done her chores each day she would go down and sit outside her cell and do all that she could to communicate with her.

She would sit outside the room, talk through the bars of the door, speak to Annie and take her biscuits. She would tell her stories from the Bible and speak to her about Jesus, telling her how much He loved her. There was no change. Annie sat in that cell looking into the corner completely unresponsive – no expression on her face, no words coming out of her mouth and no sign of any emotion. Nothing.

But this Christian lady persisted. She visited in this way for many, many months. She would do her day shift and then go and sit with Annie.

One day the Christian lady took great encouragement because she noticed that one of the biscuits she'd left had been taken! She persevered in all that she did. Other small responses began to come from Annie. The carer then went to the trained staff and said, "I really think that you should give Annie another opportunity for medical treatment. I have witnessed real progress and change."

They listened to what the lady said and took it on board. This true story says that Annie made a full, total and complete recovery. Annie came out of her world of shadows and confusion, and stepped into a world of normality. She was eventually told that she could be released from the asylum. At that point, Annie said this: "I have been so moved by the love shown to me that I really don't want to go. I want to stay here and help people just like me." She did this for some time.

Half a century later, the Queen of England held a special ceremony to honour one of America's most inspiring women. That woman was Helen Keller. She had been born perfectly normal, but at the age of nineteen months contracted an illness which left her deaf and totally blind. Helen Keller became one of the inspirations of the 20th Century and she was taken to Buckingham Palace to be honoured by the Queen. The Queen asked her, "To what would you attribute your success in becoming one who overcame the dual handicap of blindness and deafness?"

Helen Keller said this: "I would be nothing if it wasn't for a lady called Ann Sullivan. Ann Sullivan changed my life."

Ann Sullivan was little Annie, whose early life was of no significance to anyone, spent in the basement of a mental asylum. It was only because of one lady's determination and love that her life was changed. Ann Sullivan was given as an aide to work with Helen Keller when no one else could connect with her. There was no language that she could communicate in. So, over a period of time, Ann Sullivan worked with Helen to introduce a language through touch and feeling, teaching her to speak through holding her throat, mouth and lips. She patiently brought Helen Keller out of a world of complete isolation to connect with the world. One might say she repeated her own history. Helen Keller went on to become one of the great reformers of the 20th Century.

Isn't that an amazing story? One Christian woman, with no professional qualifications, took time to walk proven pathways that not only changed this little girl's life, but touched the world!

I believe that within each of us there is a deep desire to live a life of greatness and real contribution. We all want to be significant to others and to make a difference. Despite the doubts concerning ourselves and the challenges we personally face, I want to tell you today that this is possible for YOU, however you feel. I know this, because it is God's desire.

When David was able to say, *"He leads me in paths of righteousness for His name's sake"* notice that it wasn't for his own sake. In other words, there was a much bigger purpose here. It was about the glory of God, not the ego of man.

The pathway to significance is a journey that goes like this:

The Lord is my Shepherd, my needs are taken care of.

The Lord is my Shepherd, my soul is restored.

The Lord is my Shepherd, I have well-trodden pathways to walk.

The Lord is my Shepherd, now what difference can I make?

Many of us have experienced things in life that are pretty negative. However, when the Lord becomes our Shepherd we are not just taken care of and made whole, but the world around us ends up glad that we are here. We start to live lives of real distinction.

The pathway to surrender

William Booth, the founder of the Salvation Army, said
this: "The greatness of a man's power is the measure of
his surrender." The truth is we all surrender to something.
We surrender to opinions, to ideas, to ideals, to people and
the way they influence our lives. The most important thing
for your life and mine is that we keep surrendering to the
right thing. "The Lord is my Shepherd and He guides me."
It means that I'm constantly in the place of acknowledging
that I need to be led. I'm not my own man. I need a leader, I
need a Shepherd and I need to submit my life to God. I want
Him to direct me.

There is a key word here: we need to keep surrendering.
Some people surrender to Jesus in a Christian meeting and
that is great. But by Monday afternoon they've started living
for themselves again. To keep surrendering means it becomes
a habit, a pattern of life. Aristotle once said, "We are what
we do repeatedly." You and I are the result of our habits.

I'm constantly amazed at Jesus. When I read His story I
find that He's often spotted climbing up a mountain to pray.
He makes a habit of spending time alone with His Father.
He then comes back and makes major decisions. We'd say,
"How did you know which apostles to choose? How did you
know to move from Nazareth to Capernaum? How did you
know where to go where a miracle would happen?"

It's because He had a pathway, a routine in his life. The
routine was that He kept going back to God saying, "Lead
me. Direct me."

E. Stanley Jones, a missionary in India and a great author,
said, "If you don't surrender to Christ, you will surrender to
chaos." So when pressure comes into your life financially,
relationally, with sickness, confusion or emotional turmoil,
do you submit to that? Or do you say, "No, I'm sorry, the

place of surrender has already been occupied in my life." It's occupied because you're giving your life to God and you're looking for Him to say, "Walk in this way."

Some people, when they come to look for leading or guidance, want to be a bit overly-spiritual about it. They want "feelings" or flashes of light, angels or visions. Others want to be cold, calculated and completely rational; they want a scientific formula for it. But the reality of surrender is found in neither of these. It's about a relationship, about walking with God with a heart attitude that says, "You're in charge here."

I was quite impressed by most of what I heard during the inauguration of President Obama. There were many things that were said that I found inspiring and uplifting. But there was one thing that gave me great concern. Obama went to a choir and they sang to him, "You've got the whole world in your hands." I thought, "No, he hasn't! He'd better, in his heart, bow down really quickly and acknowledge that God has got the whole wide world in His hands!"

We need to keep surrendering to the right thing. It's a well-worn pathway for believers. That's why Jesus taught us to pray, *"Our Father who art in heaven, hallowed be Thy name. Thy kingdom come, Thy will be done ..."* It's not just about submitting when you have a crisis – it's a way of life.

The pathway to protection

In Psalm 91 we read,

> *"Because you have made the LORD, who is my refuge, even the Most High, your dwelling place ..."*
>
> (Psalm 91:9 NKJV)

Many people read Psalm 23 at funerals and they do find great comfort in this psalm. But not everyone has made the decision to say *"The Lord is MY Shepherd."* And to claim it after death is too late! I want to go on a pathway where I'm constantly living in God-controlled territory – in the place of His protection. It's a little bit like coming to live under an umbrella called "God". When I'm doing that, I'm inviting Him to protect and direct every detail of my life.

You will probably remember the amazing story in January 2009 of a US Airways plane bound for Charlotte that crashed into the Hudson River after aborting its takeoff from LaGuardia Airport. It sat in the river, slowly sinking whilst every person on board was rescued by ferries. What a miracle! I mean, with no engines working, the pilot managed to miss New York and its many skyscrapers and land safely and slowly in water! I'm told that one of the girls on the plane was the daughter of a pastor from a church in Western Australia. Only that night her parents had been praying and asking God to bring their daughter under the protection of His covering. Maybe 149 other people got their lives saved because of that one prayer!

The Bible teaches us that as we live under God's protection, we need to do it with the attitude of Psalm 111:10 (NIV) where, *"The fear of the Lord is the beginning of wisdom."* We don't want to make a wrong move, and we want our lives to be directed by God.

Proverbs 22:4 (NIV) says: *"By humility and the fear of the Lord are riches and honour and life."* Fear of the Lord is not about being afraid. It is, instead, about honouring Him, revering Him, respecting Him and wanting every area in your life under His care. I would be too afraid to go through this year without my finances in God-controlled territory. I wouldn't want to go into this year without my marriage, my children and the church under God's banner of protection. It's a choice and an action that I'm taking. I'm putting everything under God's covering and then choosing to live by the precepts He's put in place concerning those specific areas.

The pathway to success

Did you know that as Christians we can make it our aim to be successful in life? The dictionary defines success as, "having achieved or having the desired outcome or to turn out well". My car is successful if it gets me from A to B. The airline is successful if it can carry my luggage and me to the same place. The school is successful if it turns out good results. So, when are you successful?

The world says you are successful if you've managed to increase your wealth or you have the right titles or positions. But the definition of godly success is when we bear the fruit God has planted in us. Successful lives are ones that demonstrate the purpose for which they were called. What God defines as success for you may well be very different to what is success for me. We are called to different things and to bear different fruit.

But there are some things that are generic. When I get up, one of the paths that God wants me to take is this: "Andrew, I want you to be successful in Me today." There's not been a day in my life where I've got up and God has said, "Andrew, I want you to fail today." It's out of God's nature, His character and His will. This is not to say that we will never find things hard, or fail in any way. But God is for us. We can know that He has called every one of us, *"to bear fruit and fruit that lasts"* (John 15:16).

Some of us don't walk this pathway because we think that we're no good. We choose to believe the lies of the enemy that we will never amount to anything. We think we will never make a difference or lead someone to the Lord because we don't have skill as an evangelist. Think again of that unnamed carer in the depths of the Boston asylum, winning Annie's heart in the way she did. I believe she had an expectation that something was going to happen. She was walking the pathway of being successful.

If every one of us waited on God in this way, expecting Him to lead us on pathways of success and fruit, can you imagine what impact that would make in the world? Whatever God has called you to do, you can aim to be the best, and aim to be successful. 1 Peter 4:10 (NASB) says, *"As each one has received a special gift, employ it in serving one another as good stewards of the manifold grace of God."* This is the pathway that you're walking on, as keepers and sharers of the width and breadth of God's own gracious love.

The pathway to inspiration

When I was young I was a member of St John's Ambulance. I did all my first aid certificates and used to go to football matches to help out. I learnt how to give the "kiss of life" to dummies. But when I watched some of those guys go out to play football I'd think, "If you die mate, you're staying dead because there's no way I'm giving you mouth to mouth!"

God has set us on a pathway where we are meant to connect and relate to others. Part of what we are here on earth for is to inspire, teach and bless other people in their own godly paths. The word "inspire" comes from the Latin *inspirare* which means "to breathe life" into other people.

But we need to practice it. I hardly ever wear ties these days, but when I was in business I wore ties every single day of my life. One day, my boys started going to school and they asked me to show them how to knot a tie. Have you ever tried to do that on somebody else? It's extremely difficult! I did it every day for myself without thinking, but suddenly I had to re-remember and teach someone else. Inspiring others, breathing life into them, involves re-learning old truths or finding new ones. It is about sharing with others what we have found out for ourselves.

When I set out to inspire others I'm actually helping myself too. I'm also walking along a pathway that will take everybody forward into a great place with God. When a new member is received in the Chinese Church, many of the congregations have a phrase that goes like this: "Jesus now has a new pair of eyes to see with, a new pair of ears to listen with, new hands to help with and a new heart to love with." Even if you've only been going to church for two weeks you've already got something that you can help and inspire somebody else with. Maybe you haven't realised that you can live a life that is inspirational. Start believing from today!

One unnamed Christian lady changed the life of Annie Sullivan. Annie Sullivan went on to inspire and aid Helen Keller. Helen Keller in turn changed so many things for the disabled, especially the blind and the deaf, in our world. To inspire you, here's a list of some of her major achievements:

Helen Keller's International Organisation specialises in research into vision, eyesight and nutrition.

Helen was a founder member of the American Civil Liberties Association whose campaign for freedom rejoiced as a black man took his place in the White House .

She was friends with some incredibly influential people. Among them, Alexander Graham Bell, whom she helped in his development of the telephone.

She spoke out against the degradation of women and issues that drove many into a life of shame – sometimes prostitution, highlighting the problem that blindness could be caused if syphilis was contracted.

In 1964 President Johnson awarded her the Presidential Medal of Freedom.

She spent the last years of her life, living until she was 88, raising funds for the American Institute for the Blind.

Her story has been made into movies, Broadway plays, television documentaries and over fifty books.

In 1999 she was in Gallup's top list of the most widely-admired people of the 20th Century.

Who knows who you could inspire and influence? The Queen said on Christmas Day 2008 that she, like millions of people, personally found encouragement and inspiration in Jesus of Nazareth who every day decided He was going to walk God's proven pathways. One of those pathways was to inspire and breathe life and hope into other people. Today, more than 2.5 billion people are saying that He has inspired them.

The Lord is our Shepherd. He does lead and guide us, but He also takes us along tracks of righteousness for His name's sake. The outcome is that when we walk these pathways it's not just our lives that are shaped and blessed. His name is made famous because we've decided we're not going to leave this world the same way we found it.

How are you using the pair of eyes He sees with, the pair of ears He listens with, the pair of hands He helps with and the heart He loves with in you for His Name's sake?

Lets choose again today to find those well-trodden tracks of righteousness for ourselves and for others.

5 Shadows Are Not The Real Thing

You may well have heard this psalm read at a funeral, but it is far from just a psalm for the bereaved! It is very much a passage of Scripture for the living who may feel at times as if they are dying.

> *"Even though I walk*
> *through the valley of the shadow of death,*
> *I will fear no evil,*
> *for you are with me;*
> *your rod and your staff,*
> *they comfort me."*
>
> (Psalm 23:4 NIV)

Walking through the valley

We have noticed that David describes a journey in this psalm – one that takes him from the "green pastures" and "still waters" to the "valley of the shadow of death" mentioned above. But notice that he doesn't stay in the valley. He comes through it and continues travelling. So, this verse is an episode, a season, a period in life. It is not a place where David is meant to dwell for long. Like him, we have to learn how to keep on keeping on!

It is helpful to remember that the Bible often uses the word "valley" as an illustration of the points of trial, uncertainty or insecurity we can face. Maybe you know what it is to feel like this? Maybe there is pain or anxiety troubling you at the moment. Perhaps you feel you are stumbling around and have no idea of the way forward. Notice the truth today that it is God's intention that we keep on walking and travel through such times.

Valleys in life are inevitable. David's words are, *"Even though I walk through the valley,"* not "If I perhaps walk through it." Valley times are part of experiencing life itself. They are impartial. No matter how much money you have, how nice you are, how many prayers you pray or how many children you sponsor in India, you're going to face a valley from time to time! But you need to remember when you come to a valley, it is meant to be temporary. You are supposed to keep walking, not set up camp or settle down in the gloom.

Some people are what I call "valley people". They find their identity from the valleys they've been through. The valley has so affected them that they've become "valley-like" in their thinking. Have you fallen into this trap? Have you become someone who labels themselves by the bad things that have troubled you? God has called us to be "mountain-top" people, not valley people!

The purpose of the valley

We are meant to walk through valleys for a reason. Valley times can draw out our faith, so that we are never the same again. We go on from the valley to achieve, receive and accomplish greater things; we become bigger people.

I'm told that, apparently, David had a real valley in mind. It's a great, narrow canyon situated between Jericho and

Jerusalem. It is so steep, with huge cliffs either side, that there is only one short moment in the day, when the sun is at its highest, that light penetrates its floor. For the rest of the time, the whole area remains in shadows. The road that travels through this valley is the same one Jesus speaks of in the parable of the Good Samaritan in Luke 10:30. It was a notorious road for thieves and also for predators who hid in the shadows.

Israel is a dry country and watering holes and oases were vital for shepherds to keep their flocks healthy. The shepherd's responsibility was to lead the sheep from one oasis, one piece of green pasture, to another. To do so often meant going through a valley to get there. They didn't get taken through the valley simply for the "experience", but as a necessity to get somewhere else – to reach their destiny. The valley is never your destiny, but it may be a necessary crossing point to it. Some, unwilling to enter, don't get there; others decide to make the valley their home and they don't get there either.

The shadow in the valley

We need to understand that the Bible is speaking here about the *shadow* of death, not death itself. We can miss that if we are not careful. *"Even though I walk through the valley of the shadow of death"* (Psalm 23:4 NIV).

Have you ever done shadow puppets with your hands? Shadows are always bigger than the reality. They loom large, but are not an accurate representation of size, especially at certain times of the day. Shadows cannot hurt us and they only exist because there is a light somewhere.

But when we hit valley experiences, the shadows can overtake our minds and emotions and make things around us feel hopeless. The valley produces shadows of, "What will people think? How will I get through this? How will I cope with the change? Where will the money come from? What will my family do?" All kinds of thoughts, fears and phobias begin to grow in these shadow moments. But they are only a shadow. And we must recognise them as such.

Do you remember the comedian Brian Connolly who was on television a few years ago? In part of his act he pulled a puppet out of a desk and began attacking it with a hammer. The audience were visibly shocked, but he turned to them and said, "It's only a puppet!" In the same way we need to say to ourselves when we are in a valley time, "Well, it's only a shadow!" We may also need to remind ourselves that the shadow is only there because there is a light source at work. Where is the good Shepherd in this shadow? What light is He throwing onto the situation I am in?

The valley of death

I know death is very real. We need to stop and talk about it for a moment. The Bible teaches us that, *"It is appointed for men to die once, but after this the judgment"* (Hebrews 9:27 NKJV). It is a moment that is unavoidable. But Jesus said to those people who received Him and believed in Him, that He would give them the gift of eternal life and they would never die. John 5:24 says:

> *"I tell you the truth, whoever hears my word and believes Him who sent me, has eternal life and will not be condemned; he has crossed over from death to life."*
>
> (NIV)

My brother was a heavy smoker. Whilst he was very talented and gifted, he was an unhappy soul for most of his life. He was very successful in his job, but didn't really find fulfilment in it. He ended up divorced and miserable. He had no belief in God, had major issues with Christians and thought I was nuts for doing what I was doing. But three months before he died, he met Jesus. His whole life changed. Two days before his death, I was talking to him and he said, "Can you see what I can see?"

"No, what can you see?" I replied.

"I can't tell you, but it is amazing," he answered. He kept looking intently past me.

I said, "Tell me ..."

He said, "I can't tell you, I'm not allowed to."

My step-father, who was eighty-three years of age, and had hardly ever been unwell in his life, suddenly found himself seriously ill in hospital. His Christian friends were praying for his healing but he was agitated. "I don't want to get healed," he said to me. "I want to go home. This is the moment for me."

"Is that what you want?" I replied.

"Yes," he said.

"So let's pray then that God will take you," I answered.

So we began to pray. He thanked my mother for the twelve amazing years they had shared together. In the middle of the conversation he turned, looked at the wall and said, "I'll be ready at 7:30, Lord!" then carried on the conversation.

He then said to me, "Can you see what I can see?"

I thought, "I've heard these words before!"

"No," I said, "what can you see?"

He said, "It's amazing, but I can't tell you."

At 7:30pm I was beside his bed and he was chatting away, then he fell asleep. But the very next day at 7:30am, on the button, he went to be with the Lord.

This is what I'm convinced of: the Bible teaches us that death is not just an event but a person, a demonic power. But for a believer, for a Christian, for a person who knows

Jesus before death, death has no "sting" (see 1 Corinthians 15:55). My experience tells me that before death itself has the chance to impact your body, either Jesus Himself or an angel comes and says, "Time to go!" and so you don't see death. You are gone before it ever comes. The shadow of it passes over you. Isn't that an amazing thought?

The fear of the shadow

Sometimes when we find ourselves in a valley, the biggest problem we face is the sense of fear the shadows induce in us. Fear can be paralyzing and powerful. When your life is controlled by fear, this will affect all the choices and decisions you make.

Let's look for a while at a man in Scripture famous for his valley moments: Job. Job is known for tragedies, pain and suffering. What caused that? Job himself gives us a clue to at least part of it. He says,

> *"What I **feared** has come upon me; what I **dreaded** has happened to me."*
>
> (Job 3:25 NIV)

When trouble hits him, he tells us that he had already imagined it coming! He was living in the fear that these things would happen. Now the Bible makes it plain that Job was an old and righteous man, but this didn't stop him from being afraid. But compare that with what David said. Job said, "What I feared has come upon me." David said, "I will fear no evil for You are with me."

Big difference! Both these men were in valleys. It wasn't that one of them had a easy life and the other didn't. We know that David had all sorts of valley moments to look back on. Enemies who hated and pursued him, mistakes he made, times where He let God down. But look at his different perspective. His demeanour is hopeful and trusting. He has made a choice: "I WILL fear no evil."

To be fair, David lived a long time after Job (who we will return to in a moment) and he had at least half a Bible to refer to, written Scriptures to turn to for help and comfort. But I sense that David was someone who made a choice and refused to fear. Today we have a whole Bible to turn to and the comfort and presence of the Holy Spirit, as Jesus promised. We do not have to live in a place of fear. Read these words that the apostle John writes on the subject:

"There is no fear in love. But perfect love drives out fear, because fear has to do with punishment. The one who fears is not made perfect in love."

(1 John 4:18 NIV)

John was a kind and gentle character, the total opposite of Peter whose attitude was, "Jesus, if they're coming to get you, I'll slice them right down the middle!" We know that Peter was true to his word. When the time came for Jesus' arrest in the garden of Gethsemane, Peter cut off the ear of the high priest's servant.

But John loved nothing more than to talk. When they sat down to have dinner, I imagine John sitting right next to Jesus, leaning affectionately against Him. "Oh Jesus, that's amazing ... that's fantastic!" we can imagine him saying. Then there came that terrible, terrible day when Jesus was crucified. Where was Peter? Nowhere to be seen. Where was James? Gone. Why? They thought they'd be crucified and beaten, killed like Jesus. Who was it that stood at the foot of the cross? It was John. Where was Peter with his sword? Nowhere to be seen. But John was there saying, "I don't

care what these Romans think, I don't care what they do."
He was at the foot of the cross and Jesus was able to say to
him, "See my mother? She's your mother now. Look after
her ..."

Why was it that John was there, of all the disciples?
What was it he knew that the others did not? Read this
verse again:

> *"There is no fear in love. But perfect love drives out fear,*
> *because fear has to do with punishment. The one who*
> *fears is not made perfect in love."*
>
> (1 John 4:18 NIV)

He's just given us the secret.

> *There is no room for fear when you know that*
> *you're loved.*

Perfect love chases fear away. The Romans were vicious and
threatening. John was gentle, mild and quiet. Who had the
greatest courage? It was John. Why? Because in his heart, he
knew he was loved. He did not allow fear to make him run
like the others ran.

When you're in the valley, how do you view it? Do
you let fear control you and take hold of your mind, your
emotions, and then your choices? Do you let it affect your
relationships, your today, your tomorrow and your future?
Or do you take a different stand? Do you, like David, say "I
WILL fear no evil"?

Often times we are struck with the feeling we should love
God more, but the real key is to know that God loves us!

Breaking the fear in the valley

Did you know that it takes as much effort to believe the right thing as it does to believe the wrong thing? Or let me put it another way: it takes no more effort to live in faith than to live in fear. Fear is faith in reverse. You're simply believing the wrong things. When I see people controlled by fear, they're always exhausted, heavily depressed, tired, anxious and often sick. It takes a ton of energy to live in fear. You have to work really hard to live your whole life like that. It doesn't take any more effort to live in a place of faith. It's simply a case of application. Where will you place your mind and your thoughts? You should never underestimate the power of fear.

Several years ago, I bought a new car. It was a Volvo estate. We had four children and it had one of those rear-facing seats so that we could all fit in it. One cold frosty day, coming down from the north on the A9 outside Perth, the traffic came to a standstill. I stopped behind a 40 ton lorry. I looked in my rear view mirror and said to Sue, "The guy behind me isn't going to stop!" Another 40 ton articulated lorry hit our car in the back, pushing the bonnet underneath the lorry in front. While that happened, cars coming on the other side were watching the crash and caused another one. A car hit the barrier and acted as a ramp for a car travelling north. It drove up this car and landed on top of our car. We ended up sandwiched in between two lorries with a car on our roof!

Sue got out and some people came to get the children out. There was fuel dripping through the top from the car above. I was stuck in my seat. I couldn't move. The steering wheel had come forward and everything had closed in around me. I was trying to open the sunroof, but I was trapped until someone could get me out. The car was a complete write

off. Finished. The two children in the back were fast asleep
and don't even remember it! We went without a car for a
little while.

A few days later, and now with no car, I was on a train
to Glasgow. As it began to move, everything came flooding
back, a sudden, heavy cloud of fear totally gripped me. My
first reaction was to get out. I pushed through the crowd and
pressed my way to the door. I just wanted to jump off! But
then a thought immediately went through my mind, "Andrew,
if you run now, you're going to run from this forever."

So I stopped. Really deep inside myself, I called on God
to help me, and suddenly the fear completely lifted. Now,
that sensation only lasted a moment for me, but some people
have whole weeks and months like that. I don't want to live
like that. And I know that my good Shepherd does not have
that plan for us either.

The Shepherd in the valley

David was able to say, *"Even though I walk through the
valley of the shadow of death, I will fear no evil, for you
are with me."* In other words, "I'm coming through this
WITH YOU. I'm not staying in this place." David believed
that his Shepherd was good and that He was able to deliver.
Psalm 91 is a whole passage of Scripture about the protection
and covering we enjoy when we make the Lord our refuge.
It tells us that if we live in the shadow of the Almighty we
will not *"fear the terror of night"* (Psalm 91:5). We are not
alone in this valley! The good Shepherd is still there, leading
and guiding us.

What you and I believe about our Shepherd is very
important. We've already looked a little at the life of Job. He
gave us a clue as to why some of what happened in his life
came to pass. But how does his story end?

This is what God says of Job's so-called "comforters":

*"After the Lord had said these things to Job, he said to
Eliphaz the Temanite, 'I am angry with you and your
two friends, **because you have not spoken of me what
is right**, as my servant Job has. So now take seven bulls
and seven rams and go to my servant Job and sacrifice
a burnt offering for yourselves. My servant Job will pray
for you, and I will accept his prayer and not deal with
you according to your folly. **You have not spoken of me
what is right**, as my servant Job has.'"*

(Job 42:7-8)

In other words, the comforters surrounded him and said,
"God is allowing this to happen. Therefore you must have
done something wrong …" But God comes and says, "No!
You should have told him different!" So, Job's comforters
are rebuked by God because when he was in the valley, they
believed and spoke the wrong way about Him. All too often
people misrepresent God.

How many of us have friends like that? When the chips
are down the best they can do is tell us God is trying to teach
us something in it. Wouldn't it be better to have friends who
remind us how big and great God is, and that if nothing else,
His love for us never fails?

Job himself comes to the conclusion that God is good and
faithful at all times. He says in Chapter 42:2,

*"I know that You can do all things; no plan of Yours can
be thwarted."*

When I look at the Scriptures I see this, time and time again.
I see Daniel in the lion's den. Did he get gobbled up? No.
I see Joseph in a pit. Did he die there? No. I see Shadrach,

Meshach and Abednego in a fiery furnace. Has anybody ever survived such a thing? No. Did they? Yes. I see Jonah in a whale. What happened to him? He came out of it. I see the disciples in a storm and the boat is about to sink. Did they drown? No. I see Paul bitten by a viper. Did he die? No.

When I look at the end of Job's life this is what I read:

"The Lord blessed the latter part of Job's life more than the first. He had fourteen thousand sheep, six thousand camels, a thousand yoke of oxen and a thousand donkeys. And he also had seven sons and three daughters. The first daughter he named Jemimah, the second Keziah and the third Keren-Happuch. Nowhere in all the land were there found women as beautiful as Job's daughters, and their father granted them an inheritance along with their brothers. After this, Job lived a hundred and forty years; he saw his children and their children to the fourth generation. And so he died, old and full of years."

(Job 42:12-17 NIV)

There was such a bad moment in Job's valley that even his wife said to him, "Give it up, curse God and die" (See Job 2:9). But the Bible tells us that Job "refused to sin" in what He said of God. Even while he couldn't understand what was going on, and struggled with his own fears, he trusted God to think that the best was still to come. Isn't that amazing? He had no Holy Spirit, no Bible, no church, no apostle, no teacher and no evangelist – nobody. Yet he still came through the valley saying how great God was and that he had lived an amazing life. He even had to go and pray for his friends who had counselled him so badly!

Will bad things still happen to good people? Of course. It is certain that we will all experience valleys. The question is, what will our attitude be to them? *The depth of our faith is determined by the depth of our knowledge of God.* Some of you, like me, have gone through a valley that was extremely painful when you were in it. But don't let it be the moment that defines your life. The best is still to come.

Nearly fifty years ago, outside Nashville, Tennessee, a little girl was born with serious health problems. It left her paralyzed and crippled. She had a large Christian family, but while her brothers and sisters enjoyed running and playing in the street, she was confined inside. Eventually the doctors got her on her feet, simply by strapping her body in braces.

Her parents took her into Nashville for therapy but the prognosis was bleak. A huge shadow lay over her life and her future. "Will I ever be able to run and play like other children?" she asked her parents. Her Mum and Dad, who knew and believed the Scriptures said, "You only have to believe the right things. If you believe God, the shadows will lift."

She took her parents' counsel to heart and began to believe that God could make her walk without braces. Unknown to her parents, or the doctors, she practiced walking as best she could without them, whilst her brothers and sisters encouraged her on. On her twelfth birthday, she surprised the whole family and all the medics by removing her braces and walking around the doctor's office unaided. The doctors couldn't believe her remarkable progress and she never wore a brace again.

Her next goal was to play basketball. She continued to exercise her faith, refused to live under the "shadow" and decided that she would reach for her future, knowing the truth that "God was for her." She tried to get into the school basketball team. The coach selected her older sister, who was pretty good, but the courageous girl was told she would never be good enough to play. So her father told the coach, "Hey buddy! My daughters come in pairs. If you want one, you have to have them both!" Reluctantly, the coach added the girl to the team, only because he wanted her sister to play. She was given an outdated kit and permitted to do the workout with the other players, but she was not allowed to play.

One day she approached the coach and said, "If you'll give me an extra ten minutes of coaching every day, I will give you a world-class athlete." He realised she was serious. He half-heartedly agreed to give her some additional help. She began to show tremendous skill and courage, however, and it wasn't long before she was the team's best player. Her side went on to win the state basketball championships. Whilst playing, a referee noticed how good she was, and asked her if she'd ever run a race on a track. The referee was also a coach for the famous "Track Club". He encouraged her to try running, which she then began to do.

At the age of sixteen, she went to the Olympics in Australia and won a bronze medal for anchoring the 400m relay team. Not satisfied with her accomplishment, she waited four more years, returned to the Olympics in Rome and won the gold. She capped the year by receiving the prestigious Sullivan Award, the greatest that America can give to any athlete. She decided that while being born under a shadow, she wasn't going to live in one.

What an inspiring story! We too don't have to live in the place of fear and shadow. Our shepherd will bring us through.

How well do we walk through the valley?

Some of us need some practical help to get us moving through the valleys and shadows.

◊ Don't stop thanking and praying. *"Be anxious for nothing, but in everything by prayer and supplication with thanksgiving let your requests be made known to God"* (Philippians 4:6 NASB). The first thing that goes in times of struggle is our natural ability to thank and praise God. It's the hardest thing to get back. But the Bible says "Don't stop saying thank you." It will change your attitude.

◊ Don't talk about your problem more than is necessary. The more airtime and "thought space" you give your problem, the more you allow it to grow "arms and legs" and for the shadows to get bigger and the valley to get deeper.

◊ Don't refer to your problem as if it's a permanent thing in your life or as if it has now become your identity. Remember that it is a passing shadow you are travelling through. The Shepherd will lead you, comforting you with His rod and His staff.

◊ Don't stop rejoicing. *"Rejoice in the Lord always. Again I will say, rejoice!"* (Philippians 4:4 NKJV). Even if you don't feel like it, the Bible talks about us making a sacrifice of praise. That's exactly what Paul and Silas found in the midnight hour when they began to sing hymns to God in prison (see Acts 16:25).

The Bible is actually very simple on this. We would rather go to church and head to the front, have a minister say Abracadabra over us and send us out fixed! But God says that it doesn't work that way. Others may pray with you, but the key is you giving thanks with your own mouth. No one can say those words over your situation and in your valley like you can.

Remember, it takes as much effort to live in the shadow of fear as it takes to live in the world of faith. You just decide which way you're going to expend your energy. We all go through valleys. It's not the absence of a shadow that makes life enjoyable, but the presence of a Shepherd!

6   *Divine Protection*

|||||||||||||||||||||||||||||||||||||||||||||||||||||||||||||||||||||||||||||||||||||||||||||||||||||||||||||||||

"For you are with me; your rod and your staff,
they comfort me."

Some Christians believe that God stands at the sidelines watching them as they go through the dark "valley" experiences that I talked about in the last chapter. But David's words here show us that God is not like this. The truth is that there is not a moment in your past life where He has abandoned you, or a moment in your present or future life where He will. It's not just the fact that He's with us, but it's *how* He's with us that counts.

I am convinced that the biggest promise God ever made was, *"I will never leave you nor forsake you"* (Hebrews 13:5).

Before we talk about this verse in particular, let's talk about the concept in general. Does God protect His own? If I put that question to a Christian vote it could go either way. Most of us have experiences that are not good and sometimes terrible things happen to good people. Then, to make matters worse, some of us have friends like Job's who say God was behind it all. Remember what we said about God's opinion of Job's counsellors in the last chapter? God was not pleased with them since they did not represent Him correctly when Job needed help the most.

But, there is absolutely no doubt that the Bible promises divine protection. Just read Psalm 91.

The only time Jesus said things might get tricky for us was through persecution for the Gospel's sake (Mark 10:30). I heard a man of God say to me once, "I am immortal until I have finished what God sent me to do." What a great way to live, knowing that in every challenge, when facing many Goliaths, God is there to bring you through! But, lurking in the back of our minds is often the thought: "I don't qualify. I have made mistakes, messed up; there is no way God is going to stand by me now. I just don't deserve it."

Think about Jacob, that Old Testament rogue. One night he connived with his mother to rip off his brother and deceive his blind old father. You may remember the story. They dressed him up in his brother's clothes, applied a disguise and stole a legal, birthright inheritance. But no sooner was the wicked deed done than his brother came in, mad enough to kill him. Jacob fled for his life. Then, in the darkness of the desert at midnight, God showed up. If you were God what would you have said to Jacob? "You thief! You crook! Call yourself a Christian?" But look at what God actually said:

"I am the God of your father:
Fear not for I am with you,
I will bless you and multiply your descendants."

(Genesis 26:24)

I find God's response shocking and overwhelming. He was, in effect, saying, "I will never leave you."

In the morning Jacob was also shocked and recognized God in the place. But what shocked him was not that God showed up, rather that He had showed up in this way – full of grace and promise.

Some people think that God is armed and has a big stick ready to beat them with. But David, the David who had committed adultery and murder, saw something of the amazing grace of God. God is armed, yes, but not to "get" you but to "save" you, He is a Shepherd after all!

Let's read on.

The weapons of the Shepherd

We may think that the life of a shepherd in David's day was idyllic and peaceful, but we need to remember that at this time Israel was an entirely unenclosed country. There were no man-made boundaries or fences. This made the duties of the shepherd, wandering the hills and the mountains, even more demanding. Predators could attack at any time. Sheep-stealers could advance on the flocks or the sheep could simply wander away. The shepherd needed to be on his guard at all times.

Notice that David is showing us here that the good Shepherd is *armed* and ready to protect His sheep. He speaks in this verse of two items that the Shepherd carries to assist him. Firstly, He holds a rod, which in Bible times was a 2ft stick with a large club at the end. Then he carries a staff, which was a longer tool that had a curved handle at the end, similar to what we would know as a "shepherd's crook".

Apparently, Middle Eastern shepherds were highly skilled at throwing the rod like a spear to hit predators. It was a weapon of assault and attack, not just to protect the sheep, but to kill wild animals. It's no wonder that David had little problem fighting Goliath! Some of us are not used to the fact that our good Shepherd is *armed*. We only think of Jesus as gentle, meek and mild. But there's a whole side of God that David wants us to recognise here.

It's good to understand too what else a shepherd was expected to do for his sheep. In the early morning, the shepherd would lead the flock from the fold, marching at its head to the spot where they were to be pastured. Here he would watch them all day, taking care that none of them strayed. If any eluded his watch, he would get up and go searching for them to bring them back.

At night the shepherd would take the flock back to a sheep fold and would count them in with his staff, making sure that every single one was back home. Anything going in or out had to pass him first (see John 10:7).

The strength of the Shepherd

Do you remember the story in the Old Testament where Joshua prays and speaks to the sun and it stands still? Do you know what else it says in this verse? It tells us that God Himself threw down hailstones from Heaven and more of Israel's enemies were killed by the hailstones than were killed by the battle of swords (see Joshua 10:11). God doesn't need saving or delivering from anyone. He is strong and mighty on whose behalf? Yours and mine! God is not indifferent to our challenges, pressures or problems. He has a club in His hand and He's not afraid to use it!

The Bible also speaks about this rod in a different way. In Micah 7:14 (NASB) it says, "*Shepherd Your people with Your sceptre, the flock of Your possession.*" I think God exercises this might and power to deliver and to save, because in His hand He has a rod that rules. He is a great King in all the earth. Your life is not in your own hands if you've given it to Jesus. Your life is in *His* hands. David took great comfort from the strength of His Shepherd. He had an expectation that God would save him! He had spent many years of his life doing just this for his own flock. He understood only too well the magnitude of the Lord being *his* Shepherd.

Even when you're facing the most difficult challenge, your heart should be full of hope, because your Shepherd has a club, a rod and a staff. He's committed to stepping in and acting when you need Him to, in your life.

The enemies of the Shepherd

The Bible teaches us that we have real challenges and a real enemy to contend with.

> *"For our struggle is not against flesh and blood, but against the rulers, against the authorities, against the powers of this dark world and against the spiritual forces of evil in the heavenly realms."*
>
> (Ephesians 6:12 NIV)

Every day there is a spiritual contest for our lives and we have to decide who we are going to trust. It's a good job that our Shepherd is fully armed and prepared for that battle! I'm not just talking about eternity, or about Heaven or Hell, I'm referring to the battle for your marriage, for your finances and for your whole journey and life as a Christian.

Jesus said this: *"The thief comes only to steal and kill and destroy"* (John 10:10 NIV). Who is He talking about here? Jesus is referring, of course, to our enemy, the devil. Let me just make this as clear as I can. The devil is a created being. Therefore, he can only be in one place at a time. He's not God; he's not omnipresent. But the Bible tells us that at least a third of the angels of Heaven chose to follow him. He has a whole army, which we call demons, committed to causing spiritual problems. This army tries to attack us by restricting our influence, halting our effectiveness, and damaging both the Church and us as individuals.

We can live as good a Christian life as we can, but unless we understand the importance of the spiritual realm, we will never defeat the plans of the enemy in our lives. Good leadership, great character and the importance of serving, are not enough. The Bible tells us that whilst the enemy is a thief whose sole aim is to "steal, kill and destroy", we do not need to fear him. The second half of this same verse says, *"But I have come that they may have life, and have it to the full"* (John 10:10). In other words, the good Shepherd is on the attack!

When David speaks about the Shepherd, armed with a club and a staff, he is talking about an armed Saviour. He wants us to see the Shepherd as an attacking force, who is using both of these weapons, which compliment each other, to take us through a successful spiritual battle and come through valiantly.

2 Corinthians 2:14 says *"But thanks be to God, who always leads us in triumphal procession in Christ and through us spreads everywhere the fragrance of the knowledge of Him."* In other words, God goes ahead of us declaring our victory. We have already won!

As I said at the end of the last chapter, the key to coming through the valley is not the absence of a shadow, but the presence of a Shepherd. This is what God is teaching David, and this is what we need to learn too.

I had a cousin who was a sheep farmer. I remember as a child, two or three times a year, going to help out with sheep-dipping. They would funnel hundreds of sheep into a pen, down a one-way system, into a deep tank. A sheep would come and I would push it into the tank and out the other side. The sheep were dipped because it killed every parasite and insect, every horrible thing that would try to live in its wool or on its skin. Before anything could attack the sheep, the sheep dip killed it off.

The Good Shepherd is like this too. He has a weapon to defend us and another to steer us, all for our good. This is part of the concept some people call "spiritual warfare". But how do we truly overcome the enemy? The good news is that Jesus said He would build His Church in such a way that not even the gates of hell would prevail against it (Matthew 16:18). He wasn't just on the defensive, He was attacking, taking the battle into hell's territory. You yourself also need to take ground. If you don't go on the offensive and simply take a defensive position in your life saying, "I'll just be a Christian and go to church and do what I have to do ..." then the enemy will move in on territory that belongs to you.

The story of David and Goliath is an awesome tale, but it should never have happened. The Bible says that the Philistines moved in on Judah – a territory owned by God's people – yet they did nothing about it. In fact, they gave more and more ground until Goliath himself came and for forty days and forty nights taunted the armies of Israel. It took David to deal with the issue. He understood the spiritual dynamics at play. He knew that he came against Goliath in the mighty name of God. Although he was still just a boy, he understood that the battle was not just about "flesh and blood". A deeper spiritual dimension was at work.

Guys, in particular, need to pay attention to this. As men we tend to be very rational. We calculate things and make a decision accordingly. We don't always think on a spiritual level. Women are often more able to be discerning about things of a spiritual nature because they use more intuition.

We need to work together as the people of God and keep ourselves in balance.

The alignment of the Shepherd

There is a spiritual battle going on and the way to overcome it is not just through good leadership, godly character, or being part of the right small group at church. It is about the use and power of spiritual weapons: the rod and staff of the Shepherd. These weapons work in two ways to accomplish one thing: *alignment.* God's heart for you and me is that we become totally in line with Him.

Alignment means to "arrange in a straight line and make fit for use". It encompasses the taking of a side, gathering together or straightening up. The staff was used to bring sheep back into safety and to keep them in a good place. God wants you to align with Him. Why? Because, when we line ourselves up with Him, situations change. Prayers get answered because we are praying what is already on God's heart.

The Bible teaches us in 2 Corinthians 10:4 that:

"The weapons we fight with are not the weapons of the world. On the contrary, they have divine power to demolish strongholds."

In other words, the weapons of our warfare are not carnal. They're not *physical* but *spiritual* things.

Maybe something has "taken up residence in your life" and has become so rooted in your lifestyle that you seem completely unable to shift it? This may well be the result of something spiritual and not physical. Perhaps you have only known a lifestyle of utter poverty, of being totally broke and in debt? This is the pattern that has surrounded and dogged you at every turn. Or maybe there is permanent sickness in your home? Or it could be that a dream God had given you has never materialised. Maybe these things are not just about your circumstances, but about spiritual strongholds over you?

God wants you to get in line with His thoughts concerning you. *"I have plans for you,"* says the Lord, *"plans to prosper you, not to harm you, to give you a future and a hope"* (Jeremiah 29:11). Those are the thoughts that God has for you.

You may think that you'd like to get in line with God's plans for you, but your life hasn't been easy and you're facing a few challenges. You've aligned with negativity and you've given in to the pressure. Why don't you align yourself with what God has to say about you instead? The Bible says that God has good works prepared for each of us to do (Ephesians 2:10). He has a significant part for you to play, even if you don't feel that is true right now. Remember that our circumstances are not always the best horizon! To get involved, how about aligning yourself with the plans and the promises of God?

Sometimes, when I talk about alignment, people get confused and say, "Andrew, what you're really asking for is not alignment but conformity. You just want us all to be the same!" I'm not saying that at all! I am asking not for conformity but for transformation. In Romans it says,

"And do not be conformed to this world, but be transformed by the renewing of your mind, so that you may prove what the will of God is, that which is good and acceptable and perfect."

(Romans 12:2 NASB)

Conformity is sometimes an unwitting or reluctant response to a mediocre world. We tow the line and just do what everyone else does, sometimes without even realising we're doing it! But alignment is a *deliberate choice,* where you see something and say, "I'm joining myself with that." Becoming a Christian is very similar. You are saying, "I'm aligning myself with Christ. I'm putting my life in His hands." When we are in alignment in this way, the good Shepherd will nudge us and help us forward.

How can I align myself with the Shepherd?

a) Understanding His love
I align with what God's got for me when I realise how much He loves me. When I understand how much I am loved, I can completely put my trust in Him. Do you know how much God loves you? Do you realise that even if you could plan your life from beginning to end, you'd never plan a better life than the one God has designed for you? Your life plan is perfect for you, because its been designed by a perfect God.

Sometimes we think that the last thing we want is the *first thing* God desires for us. I remember years ago when I was a new pastor, we were praying for people after a meeting and this girl came forward in floods of tears.

She said, "I want to do the will of God so much, but I don't want to do what He's asking of me."

I said, "What do you think He's asking you to do?"

"I think He's telling me to become a nun," she replied.

I said, "I've got great news for you. He isn't!"

"Really?"

"No, He's not. He is not taking you into isolation. He is taking you out into the world."

I didn't even get a chance to pray for her! She'd confused an aspect of her Christian life with what she believed God had for her. If we somehow believe that God's plan for us is "second best" we will always keep Him at a distance. God wants us to align with His thinking, with His thoughts, but we can only do it when we know the truth that He loves us.

If I told you today, "I met a wealthy guy last week. He's given me thousands of pounds. I'm going shopping tomorrow at 4pm. If you want anything new, meet me in town by the clock tower." Would you be there? You'd align with that, wouldn't you?

Well, God's heart and will towards us is no less amazing. He constantly wants to give to us and bless us. This is what we are aligning ourselves to, not some life sentence to permanently live within feet of discouragement and despair.

b) Becoming "lighter to lift"
Have you ever tried to carry a sleeping child? They are a dead weight because they are so fully asleep. Sometimes we are like this for the Shepherd. We have such negative views of ourselves and our circumstances that we become heavy for Him to carry and harder for Him to lead.

So how do we become lighter to lift? It is all in our attitudes.

Imagine that your church is going forward with a new building project. The pastor has stood up and said, "The other leaders and I believe that God wants us to have that building and we're going for it!"

A whole group of people say, "Yes! Let's give! Let's get involved." But some people say, "Oh, I don't know about that ... that's a lot of money ... that's in the centre of the city ... it's a nice building, but I'm not sure about it." Which type of person is easier for the pastor to lead?

Sometimes your good Shepherd tries to communicate with you saying, "I want to bless you and bring you into a good place. I've got good things for you." But often we say,

"Oh, I don't know about that. You don't know how difficult this problem is ... you don't know how long I've been sick ... you don't know my husband ..." Are you making His job harder?

c) Being careful not cautious

Coming into alignment means being able to see the difference between being *careful* and being *cautious*. God said to Joshua, "*Be careful*" several times (see Joshua 22:5 for example). He didn't ever tell him to be cautious. Being cautious is when you're afraid to step out because you don't know what will happen. Being careful is about moving forward in the right way. They are very different. One is rooted in wisdom and the other in fear. So, we don't go forward recklessly, but we move carefully, knowing we are following the Shepherd.

d) Loving what the Shepherd loves

There are times when my wife and I have to commit to loving what the other one enjoys doing. I might think, "Please, not another shoe shop! No more looking at fabrics on my day off!" But instead, I choose to think, "My wife loves this and I am making her happy by sharing this with her." She hates going round car garages or dusty old antique warehouses, but she comes because I love doing those things and she loves me.

When we aim to do this with the Shepherd, to love what *He loves*, something amazing happens. We begin to love the things He loves naturally. So what does He love? God loves all of His humanity – every soul in your town or city that is hurting today. God loves His Church so much so that He's coming back for it. God loves His Son Jesus. That's why when we love Him, we find alignment with God. We need to learn to love what God loves.

For some of us, it is a real challenge just to simply let God align us. Whenever we hear a talk about it or read about "letting God take over" we get all fidgety and uncomfortable. We like being in control. We see it as a sign of weakness to "allow God into our lives" in this way. But the thing about allowing God to be our Shepherd is that we gain so much. We do not lose out in any way. God's power is then free to work in our lives. Read this verse again from 2 Corinthians 10:4 (NIV):

> *"The weapons we fight with are not the weapons of the world. On the contrary, they have divine power to demolish strongholds."*

Don't you want to live a life of power like this? One that demolishes strongholds? I know I do!

What power do spiritual weapons have?

In these couple of verses, David is talking about God's weapons of choice. We will look closely at one of the weapons we have been given in the next section. But before that, have a look at some of these other simple things we can use to fight with.

Prayer
By waiting on the Lord (Isaiah 40:31), asking Him for what we need (Matthew 7:7-11), listening intently to Him (John 10:27) and praying for others (Ezekiel 22:30), a "prayed for" life becomes a very different life!

The Word of God
God's Word is so powerful that it penetrates to the very core of us (Hebrews 4:12-13). At His word alone, amazing things can happen (Isaiah 55:10-11), such as God speaking out the very creation of the world (Hebrews 1:2-3).

Praise

When we are able to recognise who God is (Psalm 104:1-35) and glorify Him (Revelation 15:4) for all He has done, this forms a backbone to our spiritual armoury.

Worship

We come before God in worship as His children (1 John 4:19), understanding that we can have personal relationship with Him (1 Corinthians 14:15) when we worship Him in Spirit and in truth (John 4:24).

Thanksgiving

Look at this amazing verse:

> *"With praise and thanksgiving they sang to the Lord: 'He is good; his love to Israel endures forever.'"*
>
> (Ezra 3:11 NIV)

Some people think that worship, praise and thanksgiving are all the same. But they are actually very different. When Nehemiah went to rebuild the walls of Jerusalem facing fierce enemies, he set up two choirs to sing songs of thanksgiving (see Nehemiah 12:31). That's all they did. We might be tempted to think that Nehemiah had slightly lost his marbles here! He's got an enemy at the gate with swords and spears; he has the might of the nations coming against him and he is busy ... organising a choir! But listen to this: in 52 days the job of rebuilding was done. What does this tell you? It tells me that thanksgiving is VERY powerful indeed. Look at these three verses from the Bible that speak of the strength of being thankful:

> *"Let us come before him with thanksgiving and extol him with music and song."* (Psalm 95:2 NIV)

"Enter his gates with thanksgiving and his courts with praise; give thanks to him and praise his name."

(Psalm 100:4 NIV)

"Do not be anxious about anything, but in everything, by prayer and petition, with thanksgiving, present your requests to God."

(Philippians 4:6 NIV)

Do you know how powerful thanksgiving is in your own life? Maybe you have had a relationship breakdown with someone and you don't know how it will be changed? It's going to take thanksgiving to turn it around! Perhaps your finances are at an all time low and you fear the future? Thanksgiving will bring victory! Maybe your depression is your biggest battle? Thanksgiving is the key!

The journey to our healing and wholeness begins when God brings us into alignment with Him. When we allow Him to use His sceptre and His authority, strongholds such as these have no choice but to fall to the ground.

But how do we become people of thanksgiving? Let's have a closer look at what that might mean for each of us:

The art of thanksgiving

Learning to say thank you to God is an incredibly important principle. You might say to me, "Well, I am grateful to God ..." but being grateful is not the same as saying thank you. You can have an intention in your heart of gratitude, but unless it's expressed out of your mouth in being thankful, it will not accomplish anything.

Let me tell you the first thing that happens when you face a problem. The enemy wants to stop you being grateful and stop you giving thanks. He wants you to feel sorry for yourself. Sometimes I start a meeting by saying, "If you've got something to thank God for, stand." Lots of people do and some don't. We can all decide to be a thankful person. I truly believe this is one of the keys David discovered in Psalm 23.

So, what effect does thanksgiving have on our lives? Here are some of the truths I have discovered for myself:

Thanksgiving tackles rejection

People go through life and approach it in different ways. Sometimes they try to beat the system. They become competitive, work hard, and put lots of effort into achieving what they want. But eventually this leads to rejection, because they will never have enough "wins" to make them feel accepted. They will keep trying and striving for a goal they can never achieve.

Some people try to give in to the system. They reject themselves, believe they're unlovable and hopeless, and they believe that nobody wants them.

Others rebel against the system. They don't want love. They act as though they don't need anyone and don't want to be disciplined. They'll dress any way they like and do anything they want.

Being a thankful person deals with rejection because it brings you to a different place. You are able to be at peace, realising that God has won the battles for you. So what should we thank God for? It starts with the important things like our salvation, and for the blessing of the Holy Spirit; for friends, health, food, safety ... the list is endless. Thank God that He never changes, that He's really interested in you, that He's with you, that He has a future in mind for you, that your life is in His hands, for the promises that He'll never leave you or forsake you, that He's going to provide you with all of your needs! It's going to immediately deal with all the rejection issues in your life.

Even thanking God for the little things changes our perspective. Do you ever say "thank you" before you eat a meal? As a child I used to think it was a load of nonsense. My grandmother wouldn't touch food without praying a prayer. If ever we were at her house, or she came to ours, we knew the rule was not to begin eating until Grandma had prayed. But it's now my habit too. I won't eat without saying thank you. I've leant the importance of thanking God for everything.

I remember a few years back we had the speaker and writer RT Kendall visit us. I had dinner with him one evening. Sometimes when you've got an older, distinguished person with you, you don't quite know who should take the lead. So, the food came and I thought that he'd pray over the food. But he thought I would bless the food, so there was an awkward moment. Then he stood, in a full restaurant, and said, "Alright then, if you're not going to thank God, I will!" He went on his knees in the middle of the floor and lifted his hands in the air, thanking God for the food. He's quite a character! Being a person of thanksgiving, in the big and small things of life, leaves no room for fear of what others may think. It deals head on with that kind of rejection.

Thanksgiving establishes identity

I'm able to thank God because I have an assurance in my heart. I wasn't always like this though. When I first heard the Gospel and the pastor asked if anyone wanted to give their life to Jesus, I put my hand up every single week for about six months! I wasn't sure God had heard me. I could never, in that six month journey, say, "I want to thank You for my salvation," because I didn't think I was saved.

There is not a day that goes by now that I don't thank God for my salvation. I find His plans for me so amazing. I can come with all my imperfections and stand before Him knowing His forgiveness and promises are mine. *This is who I am:* an accepted and forgiven child of God. Do you know who *you* are in Christ? How does this affect the way you live?

Thanksgiving affirms our relationship with God

I've got five children. Two got married last year. They have moved out and have their own homes and their own fridges! But when they come to my house they walk straight past me. Guess what question they ask? "What's in the fridge, Dad?"

Now, I don't get all shirty. These are my children and what is mine is theirs too. You know what? In the same way, God is my Dad and yours too. He expects me to come to His house and eat from the larder of His Word. Thanksgiving changes the basis of my relationship with God from fear to faith. Thanksgiving also brings me to a place of total confidence with Him.

Thanksgiving leads to maturity

The Bible teaches us that the real battle in your life is for your mind. Lose that battle and you lose your life (see Romans 12:2). Regular thanksgiving is a discipline of the mind; it's a choice that you're making. People who will not assume responsibility for their thoughts cannot be discipled into maturity. Instead, the chaos around them gets a hold on them. When a person says, "I don't care about the chaos or how I'm feeling, but I am going to constantly, habitually, thank God", things change! Psalm 50:23 says,

"He who sacrifices thank offerings honours me, and he prepares the way so that I may show him the salvation of God."

If we thank our Shepherd, we not only honour Him, but we allow Him to prepare the next stage of the journey for us towards His salvation. He provides us with a way out!

Thanksgiving leads to better relationships

Have you ever realised that thankful people are easier to get along with? When we are able to appreciate what God and others have done for us, we raise the tone of every conversation and every meeting. This doesn't mean we never say a negative word, but we learn to give space to others when they fail. Grateful people make for brilliant relationships. Proverbs 15:30 says, *"A cheerful look brings joy to the heart, and good news gives health to the bones."* How do you come across to others? Are you always moaning about your life and dragging others down? Or are you the type of person who brings joy and good news wherever you go?

Thanksgiving makes us agreeable to God

There's a lovely story in the book of Genesis about a man called Enoch, who at the age of 65 had a child whose name was Methuselah. The Bible says that in the year his son was born, Enoch began to *"walk with God."* Hebrews 11 writes about him, saying, *"he was pleasing to God"* (Hebrews 11:5 NASB). The word "pleasing" simply means that he was in agreement.

The last but one book in the Bible, Jude, tells us of Enoch's prophecy. It says that Enoch saw, *"the Lord ... with ten thousand of His saints"* (Jude 1:14 NKJV). This man didn't just see the incarnation, crucifixion and the first coming of

Jesus: he saw the second coming of Jesus and the triumphant Church too! Enoch was so aligned to God that he began to share the huge eternal secrets of his Heavenly Father.

I think that one day maybe God said, "Enoch, I've told you too much. I can't let you go back now, you'd better stay with me." The Message version of the Bible describes it like this: *"Enoch walked steadily with God. And then one day he was simply gone: God took him."* So Enoch did not actually die. He was just taken from Earth into Heaven. Why? Because his life was so in agreement with God's heart.

Thanksgiving brings you to a place where you are in agreement with God despite the shadows, valleys, problems and darkness of life.

Becoming a thankful person

It's never too late to start! You can begin a life of thankfulness to God today. As we use thanksgiving as part of our spiritual warfare, then the Bible declares, *"This is the victory that has overcome the world, even our faith"* (1 John 5:4 NIV).

7 *Eat Your Way Out Of Trouble*

The shepherd prepares the best food

You will really, really want to read this chapter through!

We have already said that shepherding is the highest form of leadership known to man. Shepherds assume a level of responsibility that other leaders, mentors or coaches will not.

Shepherds also make sure there is food for the sheep, which is a good job since sheep tend to do nothing but eat. But here is a thought: God wants you to *eat your way out of trouble!*

We read that, *"He prepares a table for me in the presence of my enemies."*

Don't you run from your enemies?

Or maybe hide from your enemies?

Or maybe fight your enemies?

But eat your way out of trouble, in front of your enemies? That would put me off my food!

You may be the nicest guy in the world, but you will still have enemies – enemies of sickness, debt, doubt or fear to name but a few. So what's this David said: God puts on a meal, no, a banquet, in the presence of my enemies? God is inviting me to eat my way out of trouble?

Of course, we are not talking about grass or even a beef steak. God is a relational God. Can you imagine that? He wants us to know Him, *really* known Him. And when God comes to relationships He doesn't hold back, He gives everything.

When Sue and I married we gave ourselves to each other – not like the old joke, what's yours is mine and what's mine is my own! – we exchanged vows with witnesses present. They heard us and so did God. For almost 30 years we have kept doing this, giving ourselves to each other. It all started with promises that said, "For better or worse, for richer or poorer, in sickness and in health ..." In the same way, God gives Himself in relationship by making and keeping promises by His Word, and this Word is described as food of the best kind. Jesus, quoting the Old Testament, said,

"Man cannot live by bread alone but by every word that proceeds out of the mouth of God."

(Matthew 4:4)

And on another occasion He described Himself as *The Bread of Life* and challenged everyone to come and "eat Him", at which point most people left Him because they didn't understand what He meant!

God gives Himself to us in promises. We eat them, just like food, and overcome our enemies in the process.

I'm not the first to tell you how amazing God's promises are. Just look at what other famous leaders have said:

"The promises of God are just as good as ready money any day."—Billy Bray

"We are not taking any risks when we step out on the word of God."—Vance Havner

"God never promises more than he can perform."—Matthew Henry

"My future is as bright as the promises of God."—Adoniram Judson

"Learn to put your hand on all spiritual blessings in Christ and say 'mine'"—F.B. Meyer

"God never out-promised Himself yet."—C.H. Spurgeon.

"If you appropriate a promise it will not be pilfering; you may take it boldly and say, 'this is mine.'"—C.H. Spurgeon

"The Lord does not play at promising."—C.H. Spurgeon

"There is a living God. He has spoken in the Bible. He means what He says and will do all He has promised."—J. Hudson Taylor

Isn't that awesome? God gives Himself to you in His promises and He meant everyone one of them!

Do I qualify?

Some will say to me, "Ah, I know that there are brilliant promises in God's Word, and I'm sure He means to keep every one of them. But, do I qualify? You see, I have been told that most, if not all, of God's promises have conditions. To get a result on the promise you just have to keep the conditions."

Just look at the wonderful promises in Deuteronomy 28:

I will set you high above all the nations ...
You will be blessed in the city, country ...
Your kids will be blessed ...
Your crops will be blessed ...
Your enemies will be defeated ...
All your work will be blessed ...
You will be the head and not the tail ...
You will lend but you will not borrow ...

Wow! The list just goes on and on. But the promises are closely followed by,

Carefully keep ...
Carefully obey...

Otherwise, it's not the blessings we receive but the curses. For most folks, it ends right there! They try so hard to keep the conditions, but at best are never sure if they have done enough. At worst, they *know* they didn't make it.

So, what now?

I have the most amazing news for you: YOU DO QUALIFY!

Too many Christians read the Old Testament as if they live in that time. They read the promises then the conditions and try so hard, but fail, and feel bad about failing.

But you don't live in that era, something has happened between then and now – the most significant act in history. Jesus came and died on a cross for the sins of the whole world – all of them, every one you will ever commit – and rose from the dead to make sure you get what He came to give you.

No one can perfectly meet all the conditions, but Jesus can and did! When you accept Christ, your life is hidden in Him. A transfer takes place: it's like you get Jesus' DNA, fingerprints and retina scan. When Heaven wants to open its treasures to you, here on earth, you have to pass the biometric tests and only Jesus, the perfect One, qualifies. But if you are in Christ, you pass right in as if you are Him!

I have never counted all the promises in the Bible. Some say there is one for every single situation in life. Others say there is one for each day of the year. Still others say there are over 3,000. But look at what Paul said:

*"For as many as may be the promises of God, in Him
they are YES, wherefore by him is our amen (so be it-and
I agree) to the glory of God through us."*
                                          (2 Corinthians 1:20)

In Christ you qualify. So go ahead, eat your way out of
trouble. Just like Spurgeon said: "If you appropriate a
promise it will not be pilfering; you may take it boldly and
say, 'this is mine.'"

I know what some of you are thinking: this is opposite to
everything I have ever been taught! I can read the conditions
too, they are right there, for example:

*"Bring the whole tithe into the storehouse that there
may be food in my house. Test me in this, says the Lord
Almighty, and see if I will not throw open the floodgates
of heaven and pour out such a blessing that you will not
have enough room for it."*
                                          (Malachi 3:10)

It's there: the promise with the condition. Isn't it? No,
you're wrong! The conditions are all met in Christ! It's not a
condition it's an *application.* Many of God's promises have
to be put into action. We are not supposed to just confess
them, we are to put them into practice. God shows us how
with an *application.*

BMW may say your car will do 140mph. But sitting in
it won't get it anywhere. I could sit in one all day and say,
"I believe this car will do 140mph," but it will go nowhere.
I have to engage the engine, press the throttle, and move
before BMW can be proven right, and it will reach those
speeds on the German Autobahns.

In Christ every single promise is a yes! But we need to
apply them.

God said,

"I am the God that heals you."

(Exodus 15:26)

Ok, what's the application?

"Lay hands on the sick" or "Call for the elders of the church."

(James 5:14)

Geoffrey B. Wilson said, "Christ is the fulfiller and fulfilment of all the promises of God because he is the sum and substance of them." I don't know what situation you are facing right now, but there is a promise tailor-made for it *and you qualify*. Put your faith into action and look for the application to turn on the power!

The Bible, and particularly the Old Testament, is full of feasts and parties. In fact, God ordered His people to have special food and celebrations regularly, as part of their individual and communal worship and service to Him. There's one such feast described in the book of Esther. It looked like the whole Jewish race was going to be wiped out, but, through Esther's faithfulness and courage, the nation was saved. So they threw a huge party and shared a big feast. Jesus too loved going to parties. He had such a reputation for them that the other religious leaders had a problem with it.

It's nothing to do with fate or fortune

Have you ever heard people say, "If the wind blows in the right direction" or "when my boat comes in" or "touch wood – it might just work out"? Or, what about the attitude that says, "We must pray according to the will of God and, since we don't know or are not really sure what His will is, then we may or may not get a result." Some think God is moody and if we catch Him on a "good day" we'll get a breakthrough. Others think, "I hope I haven't upset Him." Still others think, "My faith isn't big enough."

Listen, it's nothing to do with you! It's all about God and I promise you, HE DOES NOT CHANGE. We know what His will is – He even put it in writing!

The One who makes the promise is the One responsible for keeping it. Spurgeon also said:

"The immutable word of promise is, and ever must be, *the rule of God's giving.* Consider a little, while I make a further observation, namely, that against this no other rule can stand ... The rule of deserving is sometimes set up against this rule, but it cannot prevail. 'Oh,' says one, 'I cannot think that God can or will save me, for there is no good thing in me!' You speak rightly and your fear cannot be removed, *if* God is to act towards you upon the rule of deserving ... [but, it is] under grace the great Lord deals with men according to pure mercy as revealed in His promise."[1]

Further, he says,

"It is not your weakness that can defeat God's promise nor your strength that can fulfil the promise. He that spoke the word will Himself make it good ... The power of the promise lies in Him who made the promise."

Obadiah Sedgwick, one of Spurgeon's mentors, said this concerning Psalm 23:5:

"God doth not at all depend upon wicked men in the benediction of his servant ... Now the malice and contrivances of evil men are too short and weak for the divine intention of blessing."

---

1   *God Promises You,* C.H. Spurgeon, Whitaker House.

God is not "wrong-footed" when difficult things happen to us. It doesn't make Him change His plans. The "table" being made ready for you will not depend on what your enemies, or your friends, are doing at the time.

Learning how to eat

Sometimes, when we're under pressure and feel the weight of the pressures around us, we don't want to "eat" from God's Word as we should. But when you face a problem, a sickness, or an economic challenge, the answer is to "eat your way out of it".

God's Word is often likened to food. Psalm 119:103 says:

"How sweet are your words to my taste, sweeter than honey to my mouth!"

Eating well of God's Word brings a sweetness to life, even in the eye of a storm. We also read many verses in the Bible that share some of the blessings of "eating" Scripture.

"As for God, his way is perfect,
the word of the LORD is flawless.
He is a shield for all who take refuge in him."
(2 Samuel 22:31 NIV)

In 1 Kings 8:56 (NIV) it says,

"Not one word has failed of all the good promises he gave through his servant Moses."

Don't you think it's amazing that God wants to speak to you? I want you to realise something incredible. When God speaks to you, you become unstoppable. God watches over

His Word to see that it will accomplish His desire. That Word is not going to fail; that Word is going to see a result.

Isaiah 55:11 says:

> *"My word that goes out from my mouth: It will not return to me empty, but will accomplish what I desire and achieve the purpose for which I sent it."*

Every word that God speaks is going to see a result. I'd go as far as to say that the most important thing in your life presently is the Word of God that you are now carrying. This concept is really important for you, especially if you're a new Christian, because you have to learn to eat. Peter says, *"desire the sincere milk of the word"* (1 Peter 2:2 KJV). We all need to crave it, draw on it and get it into our lives. This is the table that God has set for each of us.

The reliability of God's Word

Some people say to me, "Well, Andrew, I'm not sure how or if I should trust the Bible." I recently heard a Radio 4 programme debating religion, Christianity and morals. Michael Portillo, an atheist, was one of the guests and made the comment, "The trouble with Christians is that they make the Bible say anything they want it to say."

That is not true! The Bible is very clear in its message and we can totally trust it as God's Word. Let me tell you a little about it.

The word "Bible" means library. There are 66 books and each one is different in its nature and purpose. If you lined them up on a shelf, you'd have history books, poetry books, letters and love stories. But all of it tells us one amazing story.

Over a period of 1,500 years, more than 35 different authors, inspired and carried along by the Holy Spirit, wrote the book we now have today. The writers penned words onto parchment or papyrus with bone quills in dim light, often in difficult situations. Even very early on, people realised that what they were writing was so precious the words needed to be written and copied incredibly carefully.

Jewish scribes were renowned for being meticulous. Before a scribe could copy Holy Scripture, he was required to bathe and dress himself in Jewish ritual clothing. Only a certain kind of ink was allowed and there were rules governing the spacing of words. No word or letter could be dictated or written from memory – it had to be read and then written. Lines and letters were methodically counted and if there was a single mistake, everything was destroyed and started again.

In 700 AD there was a group of Jewish scholars called the Masoretes who took it upon themselves to continue the preservation of the Old Testament. The scribe would look intently at each word and pronounce it before writing it. He'd read the word, say it and then write it. The words, and even the letters of each section were counted and if they did not tally with the original, the work would be started again. We still have these Masoretic texts around today.

In 1948, an amazing discovery was made in the Qumran Valley of the Dead Sea Region. A goat herder went into a cave to retrieve a lost animal and there found a number of large earthenware lidded jars. He opened the lids and found manuscripts inside. These "Dead Sea Scrolls" are now in air-conditioned units in Jerusalem University. They turned out to be manuscripts dating back to 200–300 BC, and they included, amongst other things, the Book of Isaiah. When these manuscripts were compared to the originals, they were 99.999% exactly the same, confirming the astounding accuracy of Scripture.

Not only was the original Hebrew text copied in that way, but in 250 BC a Greek copy of the Old Testament was made in Alexandria in Egypt. It became known as the "Septuagint" because 70 scholars worked on the translation from the Hebrew into Greek. The early Christian Church would have known and read that version, including Jesus Himself.

In 400 AD, Jerome translated the Vulgate Bible and people used this Latin edition for a many years. In the 14th Century a man called Wycliffe and later a 16th Century scholar and translator called Tyndale, felt it was important to translate the Bible into English. Wycliffe was strangled and then burned at the stake for his efforts. When taken out to be executed, he said, "I pray that the King of England will see the light of God's truth."

In 1611, the King James Version was written, making the Bible available for the common man to read for the first time. What an amazing journey those 66 books have made over the centuries! The very process of it reaching us is miraculous in itself! Lives were given to put this precious book into our hands. And what do we sometimes do with it? We put it on the coffee table and rest our cups on it, or even worse, we leave it on a shelf gathering dust!

It is worth noting that the Bible is also a very scientifically accurate book. Look at these astounding verses. Job 26:7 (NKJV) says:

"He hangs the earth on nothing."

How amazing that this truth was written thousands of years before 1530 when Copernicus established for certain how the planets and the earth move.

*"For He looks to the ends of the earth ... To establish a
weight for the wind."*
(Job 28:24-25 NKJV)

It was only in 1630 that Galileo discovered that air
has weight.

"... the life of every creature is its blood."
(Leviticus 17:14 NIV)

In 1615, William Harvey discovered the importance of blood
in the human body. How about this one:

*"The heavens will disappear with a roar; the elements
will be destroyed by fire, and the earth and everything in
it will be laid bare."*
(2 Peter 3:10 NIV)

We could talk about nuclear fission or we could talk about
global warming.

"He sits enthroned above the circle of the earth ..."
(Isaiah 40:22 NIV)

In 680 BC, God tells us through the prophet Isaiah that the
earth is round!

All these verses inspire me to believe that the Bible
does not just contain spiritual truth, it also has something
accurate and inspirational to say about our very existence in
the universe.

When we turn to the Scriptures this produces faith. That
faith overcomes challenges. *"That which overcomes the
world,"* says 1 John 5:4 , *"even our faith."* Where do I get
my faith from when I'm sick? Where do I get faith from

when I'm in debt? Where do I get faith from when I've got a business dilemma? I get faith from the Word of God! Come to the table and eat. It will inspire you, help you, equip you and take you forward.

What does feeding on God's Word bring?

The Bible says that when you read the Word you eat it; it gets into you and it causes you to have corporate and personal success.

> *"Do not let this Book of the Law depart from your mouth; meditate on it day and night, so that you may be careful to do everything written in it. Then you will be prosperous and successful."*
>
> (Joshua 1:8 NIV)

God's Word has the power to heal you. In Psalm 107 it says,

> *"He sent forth his word and healed them"*
>
> (Psalm 107:20 NIV).

Some of our friends were in a prayer meeting in Edinburgh recently. There was a man there who had just come to know Jesus, having led a whole life of drug addiction. He'd injected into his leg so often he had developed a clot. If this blood mass moved it would be likely to kill him. In the middle of the prayer meeting they were praying that God would "send forth His Word" and in a moment, with nobody touching him, that man was healed. He went to the doctor the next day who examined him and pronounced that the clot had completely disappeared! God's Word heals.

God's Word restores your mind

When your mind becomes imbalanced, dark, upset or disturbed, the Bible restores your soul and makes even the simple wise! God's Word changes your life and will cause you to grow.

I've noticed that when people face a problem they want a "quick fix". They wait until the end of a meeting where they can come out and be prayed for, not realising that they need to feed themselves on God's Word too. The Word brings the prosperity of God, the wisdom of God and the breakthroughs of God.

Have you ever sat down and been really determined to get into the Word? You get up early. On the first day you manage to switch off the alarm; the second day you half get out of bed; the third day you get up and sit down to read, and then all that rushes through your mind is who you've got to phone, the letters you've got to write, the emails you've got to respond to and the things you must do for the children. So you think you'll do all of them first, and then come back to the Word. But you never do. Ever been there? The devil will try anything to stop us feeding on Scripture. He knows that the Word has the power to create. The "Word" created this world (see John 1) and it can create a new world for you.

Logos and Rhema

The Word of God comes in two ways. In particular in the New Testament, when we speak about the Word of God, there are two Greek words that are used: *logos* and *rhema*. Logos means "a message or a report, or statements that are totally trustworthy". Here's an example of that word being used in the Scriptures:

"In the beginning was the Word, and the Word was with God, and the Word was God."

(John 1:1 NIV)

Logos, the message, is so accurate that it and God are seen as one.

Jesus said, *"I am the way and the truth and the life"* (John 14:6 NIV). If you want to know truth, you will find it in Jesus. This is where all truth is found.

So, *logos* is the revealed Word; it's the message and the report upon which you know these things are true.

Rhema can be defined as a specific word or sudden utterance. Here's an example of this word being used:

"Man does not live on bread alone, but on every word that comes from the mouth of God."

(Matthew 4:4 NIV)

The key to your breakthrough is the word that comes. What is God saying to you? How can you be in a place where the Word of God comes to you about your work or business, your health or situation?

Eating well of God's Word

"Let the word of Christ richly dwell within you, with all wisdom, teaching and admonishing one another with psalms and hymns and spiritual songs, singing with thankfulness in your hearts to God."

(Colossians 3:16 NASB)

We need to build a store within ourselves of God's Word. We need to put it into our life. That's what this verse means: let the "logos" into your life. So, how do we do this?

There are lots of ways you can read the Bible. If you have never read the Bible before a great place to start is with a gospel such as Mark. When you've looked at Mark, look at Luke, then Matthew, then John. When you've done the gospels you're ready to move onto something else. Many people find Bible reading notes really helpful. You can find some in your local Christian bookshop or online.

Another way you can study the Scriptures is by looking at the life of one character. How did God work in the life of David? What did God accomplish through Esther? How did God use Joshua or Joseph or Moses or Paul? The chances are, He's going to work the same way in your life. Go and look, go and see. Read it, investigate it.

Or maybe you could study a theme? If you are sick do you know what you should study? Healing. Don't go reading about the Antichrist and the Second Coming! You need to read about what God can do in situations you are facing. Perhaps your financial situation is a problem? What should you be reading about? Money, finance and prosperity. If you've got a problem in your marriage, with your children or relationships, what should you be reading about? The most amazing thing about the Bible is that it covers so much of what we face in life. It has a story, a proverb or an answer for anything we need to know.

There's a lot of rubbish spoken these days about God and the Bible being irrelevant and unscientific. I heard a former politician speaking on a radio programme recently. He said, "Of course, there is no evidence for the existence of God." I thought, "You liar! I'm a living proof of the evidence of the existence of God. There are a thousand things that show the evidence of the existence of God in my life alone!"

Years ago, when I was a relatively new Christian, I was a secret disciple like Joseph of Arimathea. Nobody knew I was a believer. Then I got filled with the Holy Spirit and I really wanted to tell everyone. I went on beach missions around Wales telling people about Jesus. One night we had an open-air meeting. The man leading our team had lived an incredible life and had a powerful testimony. He was really full of courage. But hecklers started in the crowd and one guy shouted out, "The Bible ain't true, mate! It's a load of rubbish!"

He said, "If I can prove to you the Bible's true, will you believe me?"

"Yeah."

He said, "Come here …"

The guy came forward and in a split second the leader had grabbed him by the nose, pulled it really hard and his nose started bleeding. Then he declared, "Proverbs says tweak the nose and out comes blood!" (Proverbs 30:33)

Now perhaps that was a little extreme by today's standards, but I bet the heckler never forgot that example! Neither have I! The thing is, the Bible is 100% true and accurate. We need to live by it and feed ourselves with it often.

You are what you eat

What do I mean by this?

When you face a pressure – when you're sick or in economic downturn – what is it you want to talk about? You want to talk about the problem. Some people do that when they come to God. They don't pray, they moan. The way to get the Word, to eat the Word, is to refuse to just "rehearse" the problem. When your mouth is full of the wrong stuff it cannot be full of the right stuff. The Bible teaches us,

"No, the word is very near you; it is in your mouth and
in your heart so you may obey it."

(Deuteronomy 30:14 NIV)

This week my youngest has not been feeling very well. He
got up a couple of times in the night. So we prayed and
thanked God for a great day, and prayed that God would
heal him, rebuking the sickness in his body. He was happy
for a few moments and then he said, "Dad, if I'm not well
tomorrow and not feeling good ..."

I said, "Woah! Two minutes ago we prayed for Jesus to
heal you. Now you must watch what you're saying. We're
not talking about the sickness any more, we're talking
about Jesus healing you and you're thanking God for
healing you."

You bring the Word in your heart, put it in your mouth
and before you know it the Word accomplishes what God
asks of it.

Action what you read

When we start to read God's Word, there is often something
we have to do as a result.

"But one who looks intently at the perfect law, the law of
liberty, and abides by it, not having become a forgetful
hearer but an effectual doer, this man will be blessed in
what he does."

(James 1:25 NASB)

You have in your hands, in your house, what has cost people
their lives to give you: the Word of God. When you stand on it,
you are going to change your situation. Here's a quote about the
Word of God. It's lengthy but I find it incredibly powerful:

"Come to your Bible in the innocence of youth, wandering, dreaming, hoping, and you will find it radiant with glowing ideals, worthy ambitions, and with power to make your most beautiful dreams come true. Come to it in the prime of life, when burdens are heaviest and pressing duties crowd your every hour, and you will find in it the strength for the task and sustenance for the journey.

Come to it in advancing years, when energy is failing and shadows are falling, and you will find in it light for your eventide, and a wondrous hope of a new and better life to come. Come to it conscious of sin, burdened with a desire to be the kind of man or woman you know you should be and you will find in it a way of escape from the shackles that hold you in bondage. Peace will come to your troubled conscience as you receive power for victory over evil.

Come to it depressed in spirit, crushed by the hardness of the way and the perplexities that confront you, and you will find in it the refreshing of spirit for which you yearn. Come to it in sorrow because of some great loss or tragic bereavement, and you will find in it comfort such as nothing else can give and a promise of glad reunion beyond the grave.

Throughout your Bible runs a veritable river of life, flowing from heaven itself. Open it, read it, and this spiritually radioactive flood will begin to flow through the channels of your mind, healing, cleansing, restoring, invigorating, with a mysterious energy no other source can supply. It will clarify your vision, correct your judgement, purify your ambitions.

Given free course, the first tiny trickles of this wondrous dream will swell into a mighty torrent, sweeping away all that is unlovely and unholy from your nature and stimulating the development of every noble quality.

Then, sooner than you think, it will overflow naturally and irresistibly into selfless service for others.

What a treasure is this! And what a pity to have it in your home and not look for it! To be poor when you might be rich! To be weak when you might be strong! To be sad and dejected when you might be radiant with joy! Believe me when I say this treasure is very close to you. You may even be touching it at this moment. It is in your Bible."[2]

Hungry yet?

---

2   Quoted by Arthur Stanley Maxwell

8 The Host with the Most

The generous welcome

The ancient peoples of the Middle East were renowned for their spirit of hospitality, taking great pride in hosting both friends and strangers. In Israel, when someone arrived at a camp or home, the owner would do two things for them: they would firstly anoint the visitor with soothing, cooling oil and, secondly, pour out fine wine for them to drink.

This is the custom David is describing for us in the fifth verse of Psalm 23.

> *"You anoint my head with oil;*
> *My cup runs over."*
>
> (Psalm 23:5 NKJV)

The oil used would have had a refreshing quality with a beautiful fragrance to mask any other aroma picked up on the journey. The traveller would then be given a cup, glass or goblet, which contained the finest wine the host had to offer. As a mark of welcome, the head of the household would pour the wine and keep it flowing.

The message from these two deliberate acts of hospitality was this: "You are warmly received, welcomed and accepted in my house and, in the same way that I have poured the wine in abundance while you are under my roof, you will have no need, no lack, and everything you could possibly want whilst you stay with me."

If a visitor arrived, it wasn't ever left to a servant or family member to show the customs of welcome. It was always up to the head of the home. Everyone in the camp would have noticed this treatment and shown respect and deference for the traveller too.

Here, David is describing the intimate moment of welcome and the depth of generosity shown by God, his Host, towards him. Note that the verse does not say, "I am anointed" but, "You anoint me". The actual act of anointing is done by God, the Host, Himself.

A few weeks ago I went to visit someone and was welcomed very graciously. After he had sat me down, he pulled a ram's horn off the wall and blew it loudly, declaring, "I am so glad you are here that I wanted to blow this!" Every neighbour in the whole street would have known that something was happening in that household!

When I go and visit my family in Wales, they insist I sit at the table and have tea, cake and sandwiches, even if I've already eaten, because they love being hosts. Hospitality is a very important part of feeling welcomed in a new place. This verse is all about how accepted and welcomed we are by our God.

The generous God

Can you detect the change of tempo that has occurred in the psalm? David has, until now, been speaking about sheep out in the field, but a shift in scenery has taken place. Now David is speaking about our human relationship with our Father. He describes the table being prepared for him in the presence of his enemies and then goes on to highlight the customs and blessings of God, the Host.

Many Christians and theologians haven't ever begun to grasp the nature of God's goodness and generosity towards them. Some believe that God meets their basic needs, but would never want to fulfil their dreams or desires. But the Bible reveals God as "the host with the most". When we come to His house, He anoints our heads with His oil and causes the cup He has given us to overflow! This is not a miserly, begrudging welcome, but an over-the top warm welcome from an excited and loving Father.

Some of us fall into the trap of trying to appease God somehow. We are so steeped in a culture that has taught us God is against us. Our attempts to approach Him often involve climbing a self-imposed kind of "holiness ladder". We think that we might be acceptable to Him if we manage not to lose our temper or kick the cat, if we read our Bibles and give to charity, etc. We fool ourselves into believing that this is what God wants, and that because we have done this, He will somehow, reluctantly, get round to giving us something we need. Perhaps we need to redress our understanding of God a little – or a lot!

I think the apostle Paul also understood the Father's heart of generosity. Look at the language he uses to describe God in his letter to the church at Ephesus:

"God ... has blessed us with every spiritual blessing ... according to the kind intention of His will ... to the praise of the glory of His grace, which He freely bestowed on us ... which He lavished on us. I pray that the eyes of your heart may be enlightened, so that you will know what is the hope of His calling, what are the riches of the glory of His inheritance in the saints, and

what is the surpassing greatness of His power toward us
who believe"
          (taken from Ephesians 1:3-19 NASB).

You can almost feel Paul struggling for words as he tries
to tell us about the size and the magnitude of God's heart
towards His people. The God we serve says to us: "While
you're in My house you will lack nothing. Everything you
need for life will be provided for you."

The Host who wants us to ask

Has anyone ever treated you to a stay in a really amazing
hotel? We were in Dubai for a couple of days last year. We
tried to get into a 7-star hotel, even though we hadn't made
a reservation. We weren't successful! Apparently, you can't
even get into that hotel without making an appointment and
it was an astronomical $32 just for one cup of coffee!

But I have been in some 5-star and 6-star hotels in the
world. Maybe you have too? The sense of opulence and the
attention to detail is sometimes staggering! Maybe it's been
your birthday and you've been given some time in a spa or
health resort? Or perhaps it was an anniversary and you went
away somewhere really special?

What do you feel when you get that amount of attention
devoted towards you? What's the response in your heart
when someone takes care of you like that? Some of us lap
it up and some of us loathe it. We don't feel worthy of
the attention and the care given to us. Some of us transfer
feelings like that onto God when He seeks to provide
and care for us. We run from the anointing oil and the
overflowing cup. We would prefer to sit in the shadows
and allow someone else "who deserves it" to be receiving
the blessings.

I need to tell you that, according to Scripture, God longs to treat you like this, not just the person next to you who looks more holy! There's abundance in the very heart of God that you and I need to grasp. Can you imagine how you would feel and respond to what is going on in your life right now, if you had the security of that truth in your heart?

William Carey said, "A man should attempt great things for God and believe for great things from Him." God doesn't want you to just get through life, He wants you to come through victorious. He wants you to feel His love, care and attention. But often we do not feel worthy of this, do we? In the middle of our challenges we are slow to ask of Him because we are not secure that His desire is to bless us.

James says,

"You do not have, because you do not ask God."

(James 4:2 NIV)

If I met you in the street today and said, "Hi, great to see you. We need to have a coffee sometime," you'd probably think it was nice, but you might not think I really meant it. If I said to you twice, "No, no, we must have that coffee," you'd think I was a bit more serious. What if I said to you not twice, but five times in one conversation? Would you believe me then? Would you think I was serious? I think you would!

In one conversation, recorded for us in John's gospel, Jesus repeats five times:

"... whatever you ask the Father in My name He will give you."

(John 16:23 NIV)

This is the God we worship and the God we know. He longs for us to ask of Him and His desire is to give us what we ask for. What an amazing truth this is!

Undeserved favour

Do you know one of the things that I love about Psalm 23? David doesn't mention any of his weaknesses, sins or mistakes. He does in many other psalms, but not here. Most people think this psalm was written towards the end of David's life when he was already a king who had committed adultery, been responsible for murder and committed a host of other sins. And yet in this psalm none of it is raised. Far from hiding who he really is, David is choosing to dwell on who God is instead. He simply reflects on "the host with the most".

We often have to battle with our minds because all too easily we can think: "I don't deserve God's favour ... I've failed in this area ... I'm not good enough or holy enough ..." We become sin-conscious, not righteousness-conscious. You might say to me today, "But I don't deserve it Andrew! Look at my life and what I've done." In some ways, you are absolutely right. You and I don't deserve the blessing of God. But Paul wrote in Ephesians that God is rich in mercy and has lavish grace.

We use these words interchangeably, but they mean different things. We sometimes talk about grace as being *God's Riches At Christ's Expense*. Do you know what grace is? Grace is when you are given in abundance what you haven't earned, haven't paid for and *don't* deserve. Mercy is when punishment you *do deserve* is withheld from you.

What kind of shift would happen in our lifestyles, or practices and endeavours, if we began to understand how

God desires to be a host, to show us mercy and grace and to take care of every aspect of our lives?

Just look at this beautiful passage from Peter:

"His divine power has granted to us everything
pertaining to life and godliness, through the true
knowledge of Him who called us by His own glory
and excellence. For by these He has granted to us His
precious and magnificent promises, so that by them you
may become partakers of the divine nature."

(2 Peter 1:3-4 NASB)

In other words, we can live and walk in this world knowing God Himself is there with us and working for us. His very nature of generosity and hospitality, care and concern, desires to give us all things:

"He who did not spare His own Son, but delivered Him
over for us all, how will He not also with Him freely give
us all things?"

(Romans 8:32 NASB)

This passage from Romans states that if God was willing to empty Heaven of His most precious treasure, His Son, this act proves His heart to pour out His blessings on us until our cup overflows!

More than enough

When we look at the stories in Scripture of where God has been at work, what do we see? Generosity on every side.

The book of Ezra (See Ezra 7) tells the story of a man who wanted to get a building for God. Both the king and the people were against him. But the Bible says that God turned

their hearts and do you know what happened? The king gave
him 40 tonnes of silver, immeasurable gold and vats full of
wine, and then said, "That'll get you started on a building
project, *and* give you something to drink! When you need
some more, everybody who works for me will provide for
you." The Bible says that they successfully built the temple.
What a story of God's generosity towards His people!

In the New Testament we read of Jesus having a
conference, a kind of summer school. The people listening
began to get hungry, so Jesus instructed the disciples to give
them something to eat. Jesus' followers were concerned.
There were so many people present that a year's salary
wouldn't be enough to feed them all. They presented Jesus
with one small boy's packed lunch. Out of five loaves and
two fish, Jesus fed five thousand men, plus women and
children (see John 6).

But what happened next? He instructed the disciples to
go around the campsite and to pick up what was left over.
Twelve basketfuls were collected. Can you imagine what the
little boy who had given up his lunch thought of that?

Another tale of God's abundance can be found in Luke 5.
Some fishermen had been at work all night and had caught
nothing, but Jesus tells them to go into deeper water and cast
their nets again. The Bible says that they caught so many
fish (v6) the boat began to sink under the weight!

Every story we look at in the Scriptures shows us more
about the unmerited favour of God for His people and His
heart of giving us "more than enough".

In 1 Kings 17:7 we read of a woman, a widow at Zarephath,
who in the midst of a famine is about to make a last meal for
herself and her son. Elijah is sent to her by God and he asks
her for a small loaf of bread. In faith, she trusts the prophet
and God answers her by providing a never-ending supply of
oil and flour. It just keeps flowing over and over.

The overflowing cup

When I look at the character of God and His Word, I see
time and again the "overflowing cup" of His blessing. When
we come to know God and have a relationship with Him,
we are given a fresh start, a brand new beginning. Do you
know what that feels like? Some of us, even though we're
Christians, do not know the truth of that at all. It is possible
to be saved, but still plagued by doubt. We can live for years
in the shadow of our past mistakes. They loom towards us
and prevent us from moving forward, releasing our God-
given destiny.

The Bible makes it clear that Jesus has given you
authority over all the devil's power. Do you know that
authority is greater than power? Authority can be held up
in a 9 stone, 5' 8" brand new police recruit who can face a
20 stone, 6'6" giant. The big one has more power, but the
smaller has more authority. The crown on his hat and the
lapels of his uniform says that there is a greater authority
backing him up. We can stand before the enemy in the
power of Christ knowing that the battle is already won on
our behalf.

It is told that Lester Sumrall was travelling through Tibet.
He stayed in a monastery because there were no hotels.
One night he was sharing a monk's cell and his bed began
to float. Spirits and demons were at work. He woke up
and said, "In Jesus' name, put it back!" The bed slammed
against the wall. He thought, "If the demon can shift it, it
can put it back!" He knew that he had authority over the
powers of darkness and that his cup of blessing was filled
to overflowing.

There are three very important things we need to do in order to live out the blessings of God's "overflowing cup" for ourselves:

1. Acknowledge our need of God

David says, *"He anoints my head with oil and my cup overflows."* God takes away the perspiration, the pressures, even the sin of our lives and covers us with the fragrance of righteousness. I am convinced that one of the reasons we don't see the breakthroughs we want is because we resort to human ingenuity instead of God's empowerment. Once we acknowledge our need of God we give Him permission to BE God in each situation and challenge!

Remember the story of Ezra? There he is, loaded up with tonnes of silver and gold to take on a four-day journey to Jerusalem. He says, "I gathered men who were willing to carry all of this treasure with me to Jerusalem to build a temple, but I was afraid to ask the king for a bodyguard. I'd already told Him how great God was. So we fasted and prayed and set out on our journey and we arrived safe and sound" (paraphrased from Ezra 8). No bandits attacked them and no hold-ups occurred because they trusted God.

Sometimes we find ourselves in a difficult situation that God Himself needs to do something about, not to show how clever we are, but to show how big He is. We need to nurture that mindset where we acknowledge our dependency on Him. Fasting, praying, attending a small group, getting into the blessings of His Word, can all help us develop the habit of relying on Him. But in the end it's Him, not us!

We have such a big God; a God who can part seas, raise the dead, heal the sick, change the weather, write on walls, create planets, and destroy the power of sin. Everything is possible for Him. We have to acknowledge that, not just with our mind, but in the way that we live.

2. Live generous lives

Do you know what God desires most of all? It is simply that you and I become more like Him. What happens to you when you begin to act like God? God begins to act in and through you. In Acts, it says that the believers,

> *"Stretched out their hands to heal and the LORD worked with them"*
>
> (paraphrase of Acts 4:30).

We have looked at God being the most generous host imaginable. When we consider that He wants us to be just like Him, what does that mean for our relationships? Surely it follows that we need to practice the kind of hospitality in our homes and churches that outshines that available in the world.

The people of God who built the temple and the tabernacle in the Old Testament understood this. When they were building things for God, they used the best craftsmanship and the finest materials. This would have been a real witness to outsiders as well as something pleasing to God Himself.

Recently, I heard Rev. Jim McConnell from Whitewell, a large church in Belfast, tell of the building of their church building which is beautifully designed and furnished. On a couple of occasions I said to him,

"How did you raise the budget for this?"

"I didn't need to," he replied.

I said, "What do you mean?"

He said, "As soon as we bought the building, I was inundated with people offering to buy the carpets, the latest TV screens, the musical equipment, offering to do everything."

There is a church filled with the hosting mentality, with the understanding of how to live a life emulating a generous God! It spills out into the community.

3. Have a limitless horizon

I don't think we expect great things from God. We need to understand that God has a million ways to provide for us. When we make the Lord our Shepherd our lives will be marked by His divine favour. As I write, we face perhaps the world's biggest recession. Whilst in the middle of it we have bought a multi-million pound building *from* a bank – it is a redundant business HQ. I have known several banks renege on deals, so it really did look impossible. Several things had to come together for it to work, but supernaturally, they did! My God is the God of the impossible. I know the Host with the most.

I have realised that so much of the Church is not preaching the Gospel at all, not the Gospel of grace that fills our Scriptures. It's preaching a mixture of half grace/half legalism. We are told that since we are sinners and we can't save ourselves we need a Saviour, and there is only one certified Saviour of the world, Jesus. So we accept Him gladly, overwhelmed that He would die for our sins, and we come to God on the basis of grace. But then, we are painted a different picture.

If the kingdom of God is like a country, trusting in Jesus gets us in, but only just over the border. Saved as it were by the skin of our teeth. As for God? Well He lives in the middle of this country, a long way away. Grace got us over the border, but to get really close to God, to get into His focus, to get really big things done, we must walk and work our way to the middle, where He apparently lives.

Now you are a Christian you are told to prove it, show it, keep the rules, laws and obligations. So having come to God on the basis of grace, we then switch to working our way towards favour. And most of us never manage it. So instead we hear, "not good enough ... call yourself a Christian?"

However, the same grace that got us in is the same grace that gets us to the very heart, in an instant, a moment. We read,

"Come boldly to the throne of grace where you will find mercy, and grace to help in the time of need."

(Hebrews 4:16)

The moment we accept Christ we meet the Host with the most. He anoints me with oil, so I don't smell of sin anymore. He covers my embarrassing odours. He doesn't smell them, He only smells the anointing oil. Then He pours out the wine and keeps on pouring. While I'm in His house, everything I need is covered. There really is no higher form of leadership than this. This Shepherd takes me out of the field and brings me into the house.

Want to come?

9 Don't Be Afraid of the Future

||||||||||||||||||||||||||||||||||||||||||||||||||||||||||||||||||||||||||||||||||||||||||||||||||||||||||||||||||

"Surely goodness and loving kindness will
[and does] *follow me all the days of my life."*
(Psalm 23:6 NASB)

Have you ever seen the *Back to the Future* movies? These films, starring Michael J. Fox as Marty McFly and Christopher Lloyd as Doc Brown, tell the story of time travel and how Marty is the only kid to ever get into trouble before he was born! Their trips into the future mean that Doc Brown often leaves a letter or warning for Marty by the time he gets there, so helping him and assisting him in times of trouble – and, in effect, "changing the future".

The truth is, the Bible teaches that we got into trouble before we were born! Adam's sin really did affect us that way. But God is like Doc Brown too, He got there before we did so that He could help us. Since shepherding is the highest form of leadership known to man, God doesn't only send you into your future, He has gone ahead of you (and comes behind you). David also said,

"For you o Lord, will bless the righteous; with favour
*you will **surround** him as with a shield."*
(Psalm 5:12 NJKV)

As I understand it, Islam teaches fate. What has been decreed will happen. Consequently, what's the point of praying, making good choices or reaching for a higher life? Mohamed never made an offer to be a shepherd, but Jesus, the son of God, said, "*I am the good shepherd.*"

Christians are not fatalists. The future can yet be different to what others have predicted for you, or what history through opportunities, or the lack of them, has lined up for you. While many people worry about the world and the way it's going, Christ-followers see it differently. E. Stanley Jones said, "The early church didn't ask what is this world coming to, but rather said, look at what's come into this world."

Recently, I read this extract from *The Telegraph* (5th March, 2009), by *science* correspondent, Richard Alleyne:

> *"Religious people are less likely to panic under pressure than non-believers according to results of a new experiment. Tests found that those who admitted they believed in God were less likely to suffer anxiety and stress when they were asked to perform various mental tasks, and as a result, performed much better."*

Isn't it an amazing truth, that scientists have proven and demonstrated that faith changes the very way our brains function when put under stress?

I know what it is to live under stress, like many of you. When I was a child, my whole family would have been considered dysfunctional by today's standards. At the time it didn't feel that way to me, it was just the norm. Many people around me lived the same way. My father left us and as a result we were made homeless. We went from a nice part of town to the worst. My mother was holding down three jobs in an effort to put food on the table and pay the bills. Out of sheer desperation we started going to the local Gospel hall that met in an old building. I remember the people singing the lines of a song taken from Psalm 23: "*Surely goodness and mercy shall follow me all the days of my life.*" I used to go back to my house with those words ringing in my head, wondering if they were true for anybody, since most of the time they were not true for me. All we had chasing us was debt, stress and what looked like sheer bad luck.

Maybe you know how this feels? I remember, as a child, my mother telling us to be quiet and hide down behind the window, because either the debt collector or the rent collector was knocking on the door again. King David knew what is was to be hunted and hounded. His predecessor wanted him dead. David lived life on the run for years, gathering a ragtag outfit of misfits and debt-ridden people. You may never have been "on the run" as a fugitive, but you can still be on the run.

◊ Some run from their past, but the truth is wherever go, you're there!

◊ Some try to run from their age and their fears of getting old.

◊ Some try to run from responsibility.

◊ Some try to run from failure and so kill themselves trying to get success.

◊ Some run from the thoughts in their head and try to anaesthetize it with cocaine or drink.

◊ Some try to run from God.

Are you afraid of the future? The week ahead, the year ahead, the distant future, death? Remember, the big key in life is not the absence of shadows, but the presence of a Shepherd.

David is now at the end of his life, which it transpires had turned out differently to how he expected. Having lived to a ripe old age and been hugely successful and very prosperous, he attributes this to the fact that *"Goodness and mercy followed me."*

Pursued by life-giving truth

David draws out two life-giving truths for us here.

Life-giving truth 1: This psalm confirms that God is good to those who know Him.
When David uses the word *follows* in this Psalm, he is using the Hebrew word *radaph,* which always means a negative kind of following, such as being *harassed, persecuted, chased away, put to flight,* or *made to go on the run.* No doubt he was remembering his days on the run. He describes the act of God "following" him with the same kind of emotionally-charged energy. Only this time he is being pursued for his good, with *goodness.* All too often, we have an incorrect view of God's character, viewing Him as uncertain, changeable and inconsistent. If He is good, we think, then at best it is only sometimes and then, perhaps, only reluctantly.

However, as David concludes his observation of the world's best leadership model, shepherding, he points out that underlying all of the above is not simply the skill of the Shepherd but the Person with whom we are dealing. This is not a man, but God! God, who is faithful, benevolent and loves rescuing and delivering people. That's why He is the *Saviour* of the world.

Look at these twin words more closely:

Goodness
It means good, wellness, best, prosperity, wealth and favour. It is the exact same word used all the way through Genesis 1 when read of God creating this world. On each day He took a look at what He had made and said it was GOOD. Goodness

is full of life and life-giving. This is some claim that David makes. Is God following me, even chasing, hunting me down, in order to be good to me? No wonder Paul wrote,

> *"All things work together for good to those who love him and are called according to his purpose."*
>
> (Romans 8:28)

Some, for whom life has been challenging and difficult, conclude that this cannot be true for them. But it is true that, "All the wealth of past experiences are made available as present possibilities," as Jurgen Moltmann said. Yes, life is challenging, there is no getting away from it. But with God it's not meant to break us, but make us! And we make it because of God. If I go to the gym and work those resistance machines, by pushing I get stronger, bigger and fitter. What held me back last month doesn't hold me back this month. This is what life's difficulties and obstacles can do for us if we trust in our good Shepherd.

David's life was definitely not a walk in the park. But he walked as a king before he became a king. He ruled over lions and bears, the Goliaths and Sauls of his world. How did he do that? He tells us that the Lord was his Shepherd. Is He also yours? That is the question.

Lovingkindess or mercy

David loved this word. He uses it 26 times in Psalm 136. He makes clear that God's kindness and faithfulness serve as the foundations for His actions. They support His unchallenged position as God and Lord. David wrote and pointed out that it was this goodness and mercy that ...

◊ Were the reason for the wondrous acts of creation

◊ Delivered Israel from Egypt

◊ Opened the Red Sea

◊ Guided His people in the dessert

◊ Gifted land to his forefathers

◊ Is the basis for God's ruling in Heaven

It happened, is happening and will happen! What a God to know and He comes right up behind me with every good thing.

Life giving truth 2: I am seen through benevolent eyes

Britain has more closed-circuit television cameras per head of population than any other country on the planet. We can be watched everywhere we go! On a fairly regular basis the Police come into one of the church buildings we own, asking for CCTV footage of incidents that have happened outside or in the school next door. But nobody watches like God watches. He doesn't just watch us, He watches *over* us. His gaze is protective. He watches like a father looks out for his family, like a mother protects her children. The Police are not there for that reason, they are only looking for a culprit.

Sometimes, when I think of God watching me, even following me, it brings back memories, like my mother saying to me, "Be sure, your sins will find you out!" The implication being, of course, that while she didn't see all my childhood antics, God saw them all!

So many of us have been instructed to think about our walk with God in such a way, always being told God is *weighing* our actions or listening to our words. Years back many Christians had a sign hanging on their walls which said something like,

> Christ is the head of this home
> The unseen guest at every meal
> The silent listener to every conversation ....

My grandmother had such a notice. I would look at that thinking, "Does He really see? What did I just say? I had better be careful!" Of course, He does see, there isn't anything hidden from His eyes. But it is *how* He looks at us that is important. When God looks at me, or any one who has made this shepherding covenant, He sees me differently to the way I may see myself. I am only too aware of my shortcomings and outstanding issues or areas yet to be changed, but God does not see me like that!

Look at these scriptures:

"I will be merciful to their iniquities and I will remember their sins no more."

(Hebrews 8:12)

"And their sins and lawless deeds I will remember no more."

(Hebrews 10: 17)

God is not looking for a culprit, he is looking for someone on whom He can shower His love, affection and blessings.

I've had some unusual experiences in my life. I remember one incident very clearly from my childhood. My mother was desperately trying to make ends meet, so I would often come home from school and have to go to a neighbour's home as she was at work. This particular night the neighbour put her children to bed and sent me home. It was dark and snowing. I came to my house, which was shut and locked and in darkness. My mother had forgotten to give me a key. I sat in the snow on the doorstep of our front door trying to get out of the wind.

Now, we never used our front door because it didn't open very well and would stick in bad weather. We only ever went around the back. I'd been to the Gospel hall that week and heard the song I mentioned earlier. I wasn't a Christian at this point, but can remember thinking about those words: "Surely goodness and mercy will follow me". Here I was, freezing and wishing I could get into the house. It didn't feel like anything was following me except a howling wind and a snowdrift! But, no sooner had I thought this than I fell backwards through the front door right into the house. I landed on my back in the passageway looking up at the ceiling.

How did that door open? I didn't even pray a proper prayer! I complained! But it was as if God sent a few angels to unlock that door for me. Perhaps today you need to remember that God is watching over you in this way. Maybe there is something you need Him to "unlock" for you? Remember that He watches those who touch your life and He's watching those who come close to you. You don't need to be afraid. He knows your needs, desires, tears and joys.

Once David became king, his comrades rejoiced. It was the custom in those days to hunt down any remaining relatives of the old regime and kill them, making sure there would be no threat to the incoming kingdom. But David responds differently. He says, *"Isn't there any one left of the house of Saul to whom I can show kindness?"* This was not the common behaviour of a new king. But this king knew lovingkindess; this king knew mercy; this king knew that God had given him what he didn't deserve.

Eventually, one such person was found: Mephibosheth, a son of Jonathan, grandson of king Saul. He was crippled in both feet, the Bible says, from a fall as a child as his family fled from pursuing armies. We read that David brought him into his house, fed him at his table and met his every need. His disability was hidden from view as he sat at the king's table – as is ours when we sit at God's! Interestingly, Mephibosheth's name means "one who destroys shame".

He received a highly honoured position and the privilege of enjoying a royal banquet every day. Due to David's act of kindness his name found its fulfilment.

Can you believe it? This is where you and I stand every day!

When David speaks of "goodness and mercy" in some translations, the word mercy means "deep compassion". Your Bible might say "lovingkindness", but it's the same Hebrew word. David was consumed with this concept. He wrote some psalms with one line saying lovingkindness, again and again (see Psalm 136). This word actually comes from the Hebrew whose root means "womb" and the picture it communicates is one of a mother aching to bless you! We are painted such a bad picture of God in our day and age. He has been so maligned and misrepresented. But God is rich in mercy. He lavishes us with His love.

I've discovered that the Bible heroes who did great things for God (like David and Paul) had a revelation of how merciful He was. It's almost like the bigger the revelation, the bigger the life. They realised that having God's mercy over them meant that they were showered with God's astronomical grace.

God does look after His own children. Imagine your child coming home with a school photograph. The first thing you do is look for your child on it, don't you? This is how God treats us as His children. He looks for us, intentionally, to bless us. The word mercy also means "to spare, to be gracious, to show a continual regard for a covenantal agreement". None of us merit this kind of consistent loving treatment. What we actually deserve is God's full judgement because we have so rebelled against Him. But all that wrath and judgement was poured out on Jesus Christ at that first Easter. God didn't just forgive our sins, He provided a remission, a cleansing, for them. We aren't just loved, we are accepted.

I read an article in Newsweek magazine recently about a court in Tehran who, under Sharia law, passed sentence on a man. He blinded a woman with acid after she spurned his marriage proposal. Iran's Islamic law dictated that he would also be blinded with acid under the system known as *qisas* or "fair retribution".

How do you feel about that? What he did is terrible, but what people don't understand about the Old Testament is that when it says "an eye for an eye", God holds that up and says that this is what the Law says. Sharia law puts it into practice, literally. The Law says, *"An eye for and eye, a tooth for a tooth"*, but the mercy of God says, "I will withhold from you what you deserve." Our God is a loving God, full of compassion and mercy, and He diverted what I deserve onto Jesus.

Isaiah 53, strange as it seems, says this of God's attitude to Jesus on the cross: *"Yet it pleased the Lord to bruise Him"* (Isaiah 53:10 NKJV). Can you imagine that? Such is the terribleness of sin that the consequences were paid in Christ. The outcome for me is that instead of being pursued by guilt and shame, instead of being pursued by the law of "an eye for an eye", I'm being chased by grace and mercy, pouring on to me what I don't deserve.

I loved the film they made about Wilberforce, *Amazing Grace*, because of the character of John Newton. He was a very successful sea captain and businessman in the slave trade, a self-confessed rapist of the women he carried across the ocean. But he then had an encounter with God and his heart was so broken that he wrote the hymn *Amazing Grace*. He was overwhelmed at this mercy and lovingkindness that pursued him in spite of the terrible weight of his sins.

We are often so aware of our own frailty and sin that we fail to see how much God is pouring His grace out on us.

This grace isn't a dry and crusty piece of bread, but a "cup that overflows".

Don't you think this is good news?

Cathleen Falsani boldly wrote, "Most of us are gasping for air and grasping for God." I have been like that, and I know many people like that. Often we read in the gospels of people approaching Jesus and saying, "Jesus, Son of David, have mercy on me ..." (e.g. Matthew 9:27). But Jesus wants us, with all our shortcomings, to be whole and wholeheartedly blessed. He had a heart for the widow, the blind, the outcast leper, and the woman who'd spent everything she'd ever earned trying to stop her constant bleeding. When He heard those words, "Jesus, have mercy on me!" He found it irresistible.

What effect do such words have on you? Are you a person who is full of mercy too? Jesus taught us this amazing phrase: *"Be merciful, just as your Father is merciful"* (Luke 6:36 NASB). Do you show mercy? Do I? There is a world of need out there. What are we doing about it? Is my life open to those who need God's mercy?

God is more than true to His word

When he was younger, one of my boys had real surges of faith. One day, as we were going to church, I noticed he had his money box with him. He said, "I am going to give away everything I've got."

"Why?" I asked.

He said, "I want a new bike and you said last week that if you sow, God will give back to you."

I wanted to say, "Yeah, I know, but be sensible, be calm and think about it!"

But he did give it all away – the entire amount. The next day he came home from school, the door flew open and he ran in asking, "Is my bike here?"

"Well, no, it's not," I said.

"Okay!" he replied.

The next day the same thing happened. This went on for about five weeks and his enthusiasm every single day was exactly the same. It really spoke to me. In the fifth week somebody in the church, who knew nothing about any of this, came to me and said, "Andrew, I want to bless your children. Here's some money, go and buy them something." I went that day and got the exact bike he wanted and put it in his bedroom so that when he came home and the door flew open it would be there!

This is the heart of God towards you today. Do you realise that? Are you in need today? He promises to respond to those words, "Have mercy on me!"

What are you expecting today? Are you expecting that the goodness and mercy of God are going to "ambush" you and take you by surprise to a whole new level of thankfulness? This is what your good Shepherd wants you to look forward to!

> *"Our real ideas of God might lie buried under the rubbish of conventional religious notions and may require an intelligent and vigorous search before it is finally unearthed or exposed."*
>
> —*A.W. Tozer*

10 *My Favourite House*

IIIIIIIIIIIIIIIIIIIIIIIIIIIIIIIIIIIIIIIIIIIIIIIIIIIIIIIIIIIIIIIIIIIIIIIIIIIIIIIIIIIIIIIIIIIIIIIIIIIIIIIIIIIIIII

"I will dwell in the house of the Lord forever."

As we've gone through this psalm we can see it has two halves. It starts in a *field*, but it ends up in a *house*.

Do you have a favourite house? When I was a child I was fortunate enough to have some other homes to go to. I had two favourite places to visit: one was a cottage owned by my grandparents, to which was attached a large woodshed. They were quiet folk who never said much, but I remember watching my granddad chop the firewood and can still smell that freshly cut wood now. My grandfather also had a lovely vegetable patch and I remember walking through it, pulling fresh peas, and eating them straight out of the pod. There was something so reassuring about this place. Not far away lived an aunt, who became like a second mother to me, and I loved visiting her house, probably for the same reason.

King David had a favourite house, not forgetting he had built some wonderful palaces. So, which house could it be? It was his Shepherd's house, of course, the house of the Host with the most. When we talk about God's house, Christians will instantly equate this with "church" and a whole set of preconceptions may spring up. But let's put those aside long enough to ask some important questions.

146

Which house was David talking about exactly? There weren't any church buildings in his time, so what was in his mind as he wrote? We have many instances of it mentioned in the Psalms.

"I was glad when they said to me, 'Let us go to the house of the Lord.'"

(Psalm 122:1 NASB)

"I would rather be a doorkeeper in the house of my God than dwell in the tents of wickedness."

(Psalm 84:10 NKJV)

"... zeal for Your house has consumed me."

(Psalm 69:9 NASB)

"Those who are planted in the house of the Lord shall flourish."

(Psalm 92:13 NKJV)

"Better is one day in your courts than a thousand elsewhere ..."

(Psalm 84:10 NIV)

A house of history

There were three "houses" in Old Testament history that were representative of the place where God lived:

The Tabernacle of Moses
This was an elaborate tent made from expensive materials. It was portable and was carried through the desert during the wilderness years. Every time the people of God camped, their

campsite formed the shape of a cross, with the tabernacle pitched right in the middle.

Solomon's Temple

Many centuries later, a famous temple was built by Solomon. This wasn't a tent, it was a magnificent structure. The pillars were made of solid bronze and some of them were plated with gold. Solomon's Temple was so beautiful that people such as the Queen of Sheba travelled miles just to come and see it.

David's Tabernacle

In between the elaborate Tabernacle of Moses and the magnificent stone temple built by Solomon, there was another tent that became known as David's Tabernacle. Great craftsmen built the other structures, but this tabernacle was nothing more than a piece of canvas pitched on a hillside with a few poles holding it up. Right in the middle resided this box known as the Ark of the Covenant.

A house restored

Hundreds of years later God said in the New Testament that He would restore one of these structures. It is interesting to note which one:

> *"'After these things I will return,*
> *And I will rebuild the tabernacle of David which*
> *has fallen,*
> *And I will rebuild its ruins,*
> *And I will restore it."*

(Acts 15:16 NASB)

God is ignoring both elaborate structures. It is neither the tabernacle of Moses, nor the temple He wants to restore, saying instead that He is going to rebuild the tabernacle of David. Why ignore something that is so fantastic and focus on something that is so simple? What made that tent so special that David said that one day in it was, *"better than a thousand days spent elsewhere"* (Psalm 84:10)?

A house of God's presence

Saul had been David's bitter enemy. His jealousy had made him pursue David and try to kill him on a number of occasions. When Saul died, David had become even more successful. There were no more enemies to fight. God had given him victory after victory. But his success on the battlefield did not seem to satisfy him.

When we read the accounts in 1 Samuel and Chronicles, we see that David had built himself the most amazing palaces. He was living in opulence, wealth and splendour. He was all-powerful, highly-esteemed and he had everything he could wish for (see 2 Samuel 5:10). But his fame and splendour did not fulfil him.

I imagine him alone one day, sitting in all his wealth, with no battles left to fight and no enemies to be conquered, with the dawning realisation that his heart is empty and aching. Howard Hughes was once asked, what makes a man happy? He replied, "Just one more thing." There was a deep longing within David for that "one more thing", only it wasn't a thing at all, it was the presence of God. He didn't just want to know *about* God, he wanted to *know God.* He'd been a soldier on campaign, a businessman, a successful singer/songwriter, and a city planner, but all of this was not enough.

So many people are like that – they have it all and yet they have nothing.

We know that God is omnipresent. He is everywhere. But in Old Testament times God made Himself locatable since Jesus hadn't come yet. We read of the Ark of the Covenant, a box made of acacia wood and overlaid with gold. It was beautiful in itself, but it was highly symbolic. It represented nothing less than the very presence and majesty of Yahweh, Israel's true God. David understood that true happiness and fulfilment in life didn't depend on circumstances but on a relationship. It depended on the proximity and presence of God in his life. So he decided to retrieve the Ark and bring it back to the city – and since the old tabernacle of Moses was long gone, David wanted to build a house to make a home for this ark – a place he could visit, frequently.

All over the planet wealthy people, poor people, influential people, young people and older people are awakening. More people will come to Christ this week than at any other point in history – ever! There is really only one Church on the planet and that Church is in revival! People are seeking God for themselves. They want to bring the "Ark" of His presence into their own lives.

A house of God's power

Since the Ark resided elsewhere, and there was no permanent home for it, David, who never thought small about anything, determined to build something elaborate and magnificent – maybe something like one of our cathedrals today. But God wouldn't let him do it. It was left for his son Solomon to build later. Nevertheless, David was determined to go and get the Ark and bring it back to Jerusalem, his capital city.

David doesn't get things right first time. He knows he wants to get the Ark back and so he makes enormous and elaborate preparations. He calls 30,000 noblemen from around the country, sets up huge choirs and a massive orchestra and prepares food for over ¼ million people. He plans a huge celebration full of pomp and ceremony. This was the biggest thing the city had ever seen. There was just one thing missing: he had forgotten to ask God how to do it!

David knew that the Ark was considered to be so holy it was not to be touched by human hands. It was designed to be carried by poles on priests' shoulders. But, despite this, David decides to have a new oxcart built to transport it.

> *"David and the whole house of Israel were celebrating with all their might before the Lord, with songs and with harps, lyres, tambourines, sistrums and cymbals."*
>
> (2 Samuel 6:5)

Can you imagine all the nobility, the priests and Royal family, the noise and excitement? But suddenly the oxen stumble. A man called Uzzah reaches out his hand to steady the Ark and give God a helping hand as it were, and in a split second he's dead, struck down for his presumption.

David was shocked, the people were stunned and the music and celebrations came to a standstill.

> *"David was afraid of the Lord that day and said, 'How can the ark of the Lord ever come to me?' He was not willing to take the ark of the Lord to be with him in the City of David."*
>
> (2 Samuel 6:9)

David was understandably afraid of the Lord. He could see the power of God's presence and understood that he had got something very wrong. He wondered how he could ever retrieve the Ark at all and took it instead to the home of a man named Obed-edom. The Bible tells us it remained at this home for three whole months. It obviously took David all this time to gather the courage to try again! Meanwhile Obed-edom's home, farm, family and all he touched was hugely blessed.

You and I both want and need God's power in our lives. But there are times when we like to hitch that power and presence to one of our "new carts". We like to add Him to the procession of our lives in our own way. We put out our hands to stop things falling around us, but we don't lift up our hearts to Him in the first place.

There are only two ways to connect with God.

Either equal to equal, we become as holy as He is. And for us to know where and what that looks like, we read of the full obligations of the Law. But it would mean keeping every part of it, including the instructions on handling holy things, like Ark carrying. Since we can't possibly keep all the demands of the Law, there had to be another way.

God wanted His presence carried on the shoulders of the priests, not pulled ceremonially on a cart, no matter how new and expensive the cart was. All of this was an illustration of the pivotal point in history: the coming, crucifixion and resurrection of Jesus Christ. He carried the presence of Almighty God both on and in His life, and through His grace we get to know and enjoy God.

A house of celebration

The Ark of the Covenant had resided for some time with Obed-edom and David had been told how richly God had blessed him. So he plucked up the courage to move the Ark into his own city.

Once again David goes for this big time. There were probably over a quarter of a million people there to witness and celebrate the occasion. Probably with more than a little sense of apprehension in the air. David had invited a huge amount of important guests for the occasion. This is a real party with the biggest orchestra the world had ever seen, as well as two of the biggest choirs, numbering thousands of people!

And what is David doing? Is he in a chariot in the procession, waving royally to the crowds as our monarchs sometimes do? No! We read:

"And David was dancing before the Lord with all his might, and David was wearing a linen ephod."

(2 Samuel 6:14 NASB)

This king David was dancing before the Lord, wearing a simple linen tunic. He had abandoned his royal clothes and dressed like all the other priests. This is mighty king David who killed Goliath; this is king David who subdued every enemy for hundreds of miles around; this is king David who had a legion of mighty warriors following him; this is king David who was living in great palaces; this is king David who wore a crown and royal robes and threw banquets. His love for God made him dance and celebrate *"with all his might"* in nothing more than a simple gown.

David shows us his heart here: *"I will celebrate before the Lord."* It did not depend on what others thought of him. He was going to praise and celebrate God for what He had done.

God's house is full of hope, life and celebration. It's a powerful, positive environment. Not at all like the experiences many of us have had with church. For too many it's been a place of correction, laws, rules and regulations. Even in the Old Testament order of things, God's house was full of His optimistic, encouraging, accepting presence.

A house of God's favour

David's second attempt to bring the Ark back is much more measured. 1 Chronicles 15:13 tells us that David explained to the priests what had gone wrong the first time:

> *"... the Lord our God broke out against us, because we did not consult Him about the proper order."*

He is very careful the second time to get things correct. He is so relieved at God's favour that after only six paces he sacrifices a bull and a fattened calf! I wish I could have been there on "Ark-moving" day! That would have been an amazing noise and the most extravagant and expensive worship.

This time David sets up two huge choirs. Every six steps the choir sang, *"Lift up your heads, O gates, And lift them up, O ancient doors, That the King of glory may come in!"* (Psalm 24:9 NASB). They then opened the gates of Jerusalem. Then the second choir sang back to the first choir, *"Who is this King of glory?"* (v10) and the first choir sang back, *"The* LORD *of hosts, He is the King of glory."*

But not everyone felt the same party spirit. We read the following verses that show us David's wife's response to the jubilation:

> *"... Michal the daughter of Saul looked out of the window and saw King David leaping and dancing before the Lord; and she despised him in her heart."*
>
> (2 Samuel 6:16 NASB)

In the middle of all of this, as David was dancing with joy and basking in the favour of God, here is his wife mocking him. The daughter of a king and a princess in her own right,

Michal was a proud woman. Her eyes were disgusted with what she saw:

> *"How the king of Israel distinguished himself today! He uncovered himself today in the eyes of his servants' maids as one of the foolish ones shamelessly uncovers himself!"*
>
> (2 Samuel 6:20 NASB)

She could not understand how a king such as David could be so undignified. Notice that she is not in the procession. She is only interested enough to watch from an upstairs window. 2 Samuel 6:23 tell us the outcome for Michal: she lived a life of total barrenness having, *"no child to the day of her death."* Her whole spirit seems to be one of disdain for God and the things of God. She was not able to enter His house or be in His favour like her husband.

David didn't care how he looked or what people thought. It made no difference to him because the Lord was his Shepherd. David was pouring everything out before his God who had poured favour onto him.

A house accessible to all

The Tabernacle of Moses and Solomon's Temple had many common traits. Although one was a tent and one was a building, they were structured similarly in that the Ark was put behind a curtain or a wall. It was locked away in a place called the "Holy of Holies". Nobody could see it or touch it. Once a year the High priest entered into this place – the very presence of God. When this happened he would wear a garment with bells on the bottom and a rope would be tied around his ankle. This was so that if he dropped down dead, his assistants would realise because the sound of the bells had stopped and they would pull his body out!

David built his tabernacle and all it consisted of was a roof of canvas and a few poles holding it up. The Ark could be seen by everyone and approached by anyone. Unlike the Tabernacle of Moses, David's Tabernacle was a place where the power and presence of God was accessible. God wants His power and presence to be available to us all.

Some of us can find that kind of access to God a little alarming. We prefer the kind of model given to us by Moses' Tabernacle or Solomon's Temple. In fact, we sometimes even try to build something between God and ourselves, a religious tradition of some kind.

Jesus once said to the Pharisees, "*Your traditions have nullified the very Word of God and its power in your life. You search the Scriptures because you think that in them you have eternal life.*" (John 5:39 NASB)

Some of us have religious habits that we just won't let go of, not realising that they are a barrier stopping us from finding true access to our Father. God wants nothing to come between us and His presence.

A house of worship

We think we're part of the music generation with people listening to their iPods all the time, but it's nothing new. Listen to this: there was live music day and night for 37 years in Jerusalem! David set up a worship band, music and choirs and wrote many songs for them. The music continued 24 hours a day, 7 days a week. No wonder David said, "I'd rather go up to the house of the Lord." That's where the party was! There were no walls or curtains, no Holy of Holies; there was nothing between God's presence and the people in the city, other than worshippers.

We as the Body of Christ should be a house of worshippers. What do we read in Acts 15? "*I am going to rebuild the tabernacle of David"* – not the tabernacle of Moses with all its rules and regulations, not the temple of Solomon with all its elaborate prestige. God wants to build us together as a people who know how to praise and connect with Him. He wants to build a people who know how to say, "We will celebrate!" when the world is saying, "Haven't you watched the news or read the papers? Don't you know we're in troubled times?"

Shepherding is the highest form of leadership known to man. This Shepherd invites you to His house, makes you right at home, then gives you a promise for every and any situation you are likely to meet. We call God's house "church" today, but it is still His house. It is where He lives. When we read earlier ...

> *"'After these things I will return,*
> *And I will rebuild the tabernacle of David which*
> *has fallen,*
> *And I will rebuild its ruins,*
> *And I will restore it."*
>
> (Acts 15:16 NASB)

...we are not expecting God to rebuild a tent on a hillside, but we are expecting vibrant churches where God is accessible. In some parts of the world they are hard to find, but they are there.

As we understand that only way to connect with God is by this amazing thing called grace, we also realise that everything He has becomes available to us at the same time.

To understand grace Cathleen Falsani wrote,

> *Justice is getting what you deserve*
> *Mercy is not getting what you deserve*
> *Grace is getting what you absolutely*
> *don't deserve*

But you get it anyway!

The nation's favourite psalm, Psalm 23, is always read at funerals because it does bring comfort to many. But as we have discovered, this is a psalm for the living, and finding the best form of leadership for life. Wouldn't it be a shame to get to Heaven and hear God to say, "You could have had more, but you settled for less."

I leave you with a prayer from Scripture that sums up the whole of this book:

"Save your people and bless your inheritance;
be their shepherd and carry them for ever."
                                                    (Psalm 2 :9)